Praise for Sonia Sanchez

"This world is a better place because of Sonia Sanchez: more livable, more laughable, more manageable. I wish millions of people knew that some of the joy in their lives comes from the fact that Sonia Sanchez is writing poetry."
— MAYA ANGELOU

"Her songs of destruction and loss scrape the heart; her praise songs thunder and revitalize. We need these songs for our journey together into the next century."
— JOY HARJO, US poet laureate

"The poetry of Sonia Sanchez is full of power and yet always clean and uncluttered. It makes you wish you had thought those thoughts, felt those emotions, and, above all, expressed them so effortlessly and so well."
— CHINUA ACHEBE, Nobel Prize laureate

"Sonia Sanchez remains one of the most read, respected, and visible figures of the Black Arts Movement."
— AMIRI BARAKA

"No one can read your work, Sonia, and not realize that you have always had us on your mind, in your heart, and in those small tensile fingers of your writing hand; in your voice crafted and designed for more than the ear: for the aorta, the spine, and the soles of our feet. You have spoken for us . . . Written for us . . . Sung to us . . . How much in your debt we are."
— TONI MORRISON, Nobel Prize laureate

Collected
Poems

Collected Poems Sonia Sanchez

Beacon Press

Boston

Beacon Press
Boston, Massachusetts
www.beacon.org

Beacon Press books
are published under the auspices of the
Unitarian Universalist Association of Congregations.

24 23 22 21   8 7 6 5 4 3 2 1

This book is printed on acid-free paper that meets
the uncoated paper ANSI/NISO specifications for
permanence as revised in 1992.

Design and composition by Michael Starkman
at Wilsted & Taylor Publishing Services

Library of Congress Cataloging-in-Publication Data
Names: Sanchez, Sonia, author.
Title: Collected poems / Sonia Sanchez.
Description: Boston : Beacon Press, [2021]
Identifiers: LCCN 2020057071 (print) | LCCN 2020057072 (ebook) | ISBN
    9780807026526 (hardcover ; acid-free paper) | ISBN 9780807026533 (ebook)
Subjects: LCGFT: Poetry.
Classification: LCC PS3569.A468 C65 2021 (print) | LCC PS3569.A468
    (ebook) | DDC 811/.54—dc23
LC record available at https://lccn.loc.gov/2020057071
LC ebook record available at https://lccn.loc.gov/2020057072

For Mungu
and Morani

Contents

from

Home Coming

homecoming

i have been a
way so long
once after college
i returned tourist
style to watch all
the niggers killing
themselves with
3 for oners
with
needles
that
cd
not support
their
stutters.
           now woman
i have returned
leaving behind me
all those hide and
seek faces peeling
with freudian dreams.
this is for real.
            black
      niggers
          my beauty.
baby.
i have learned it
ain't like they say
in the newspapers.

poem at thirty

it is midnight
no magical bewitching
hour for me
i know only that
i am here waiting
remembering that
once as a child
i walked two
miles in my sleep.
did i know
then where i
was going?
traveling. i'm
always traveling.
i want to tell
you about me
about nights on a
brown couch when
i wrapped my
bones in lint and
refused to move.
no one touches
me anymore.
father do not
send me out
among strangers.
you you black man
stretching scraping
the mold from your body.
here is my hand.
i am not afraid
of the night.

nigger

nigger.
        that word
ain't shit to me
man.
  don't u know
where u at when
u call me nigger?
look.
      my man. i'll
say it slow for you.
              N-I-G-G-E-R-
that word don't turn
me on man.
          i know i am
black.
     beautiful.
          with meaning.
nigger. u say.
        my man
you   way behind the set

black magic

magic
        my man
is you
        turning
my body into
a thousand

smiles.
        black
magic is your
touch
        making
me breathe.

summary

no sleep tonight
not even after all
the red and green pills
i have pumped into
my stuttering self or
the sweet wine
that drowns them.
                              this is
a poem for the world
for the slow suicides
in seclusion.
somewhere on 130th st.
a woman, frail as a
child's ghost, sings.
                    oh.
                    oh. what
can the matter be? johnny's
so long at the fair.
                    /i learned how
                         to masturbate
thru the new york times.
i thought
shd i have
thought anything
that cd not
be proved. i
thought and
was wrong. listen.

                              fool
            black
                  bitch
of fantasy. life
is no more than
                  gents
                        and
                              gigolos
                        (99% american)
            liars
            and
      killers (199% american)   dreamers
            and drunks (299%
                              american)
(only god is 300% american)
                              i say
is everybody happy?
this is a poem for me.
i am alone.
one night of words
will not change
all that.

malcolm

do not speak to me of martyrdom
of men who die to be remembered
on some parish day.
i don't believe in dying
though i too shall die
and violets like castanets
will echo me.

yet this man
this dreamer,
thick-lipped with words
will never speak again
and in each winter
when the cold air cracks
with frost, i'll breathe
his breath and mourn
my gun-filled nights.
he was the sun that tagged
the western sky and
melted tiger-scholars
while they searched for stripes.
he said, "fuck you white
man. we have been
curled too long. nothing
is sacred now. not your
white faces nor any
land that separates
until some voices
squat with spasms."

do not speak to me of living.
life is obscene with crowds
of white on black.
death is my pulse.
what might have been
is not for him/or me
but what could have been
floods the womb until i drown.

small comment

the nature of the beast is the
man or to be more specific
the nature of the man is his
bestial nature or to
bring it to its elemental terms
the nature of nature is
the bestial survival of the
fittest the strongest the richest
or to really examine
the scene we cd say that
the nature of any beast is
bestial unnatural and natural
in its struggle for superiority
and survival but to really
be with it we will say that the man
is a natural beast bestial in
his lusts natural in his
bestiality and expanding
and growing on the national
scene to be the most
bestial and natural of
any beast. you dig?

the final solution/

the leaders speak
america.
land of free/
dom
land of im/mi/grant
wh/ites
and slave/
blacks. there is
no real problem here.
we the
lead/ers of free
a/mer/ica
say. give us your
hungry/
illiterates/
criminals/
dropouts/
(in other words)
your blacks
and we will
let them fight
in vietnam
defending america's honor.
we will make responsible
citi/
zens out of them or
kill them trying.
america
land of free/dom

free/

      enter/

            prise and   de/mo/

                     cracy.

bring us your problems.

           we your lead/ers

always find a solution.

        after all

what else are

    we get/

        ting pd for?

to CHucK

i'm gonna write me
   a poem like
         e.e.
    cum
        mings to
           day. a
bout you
        mov
ing iNsIdE
        me touc
hing my vis
       cera un
     til i turn
in
   side out. i'
         m
go
  n n
     a sc
      rew
   u on   pap er
  cuz u
       3
       0
       0
       0
  mi
     awayfromme

my   MAN

    ca

    re

    ss my br

      ea

      sts   my

        bl

          ack

ass

  rul

      ED on these

lin

  es.   they

          yours.

yeah.

  imgonnawritemea

pOeM

     like

       e.

E. cu

     MmIn

   gS   to

        day   cuz

heknewallabout

     scr

      EW

ing

on   WH

         ite pa per.

poem

for dcs 8th graders—1966-67

look at me 8th
grade
      i am black
beautiful. i have a
man who looks at
my face and smiles.
on my face
are black warriors
riding in ships
of slavery;
          on my face
               is malcolm
                    spitting his metal seeds
on a country of sheep;
on my face
          are young eyes
breathing in black crusts.
                  look at us
8th grade
        we are black
beautiful and our black
ness sings out
            while america wanders
dumb with her wet bowels.

definition for blk/children

a policeman
            is a pig
and he shd be in
            a zoo
with all the other piggy
            animals.   and
until he stops
    killing blk/people
cracking open their heads
remember.
        the policeman
    is a pig.
            (oink/
                oink.)

Memorial

1. The supremes—cuz they dead

the supremes done gone
and sold their soul
to tar
      zan and other
honky/rapers
            They sing rodgers
and hart songs
as if we didn't
have enough andrews
sisters spitting their
whiter than mr.
clean songs in our faces.
YEAH.
        the supremes
               done gone
and bleached out
           their blk/ness
and all that is heard
is
        me.   tarzan
        u.   jane
and
        bwana.
            bwana.
               bwana.

Memorial

2. bobby hutton

i didn't know bobby
hutton in fact it is
too hard to re
cord all the dying
young/blks.
                in this country.
but   this I do know.
                        he was
part of a long/term/plan
for blk/people.
                he was denmark
                vesey.
malcolm.
        garvey. all the
dead/blk/men
                of our now/time
and ago/time.
                check it out. for
bobby wd be living today.
Panther/jacket/beret
and all.
                check it out & don't let
it happen again.
                we got enough
blk/martyrs for all the

yrs to come
          that is, if they
still coming
          after all the shit/
yrs of these
          white/yrs   goes down

personal letter no. 2

i speak skimpily to
you about apartments i
no longer dwell in
and children who
chant their dis
obedience in choruses.
if i were young
i wd stretch you
with my wild words
while our nights
run soft with hands.
but i am what i
am. woman. alone
amid all this noise.

2

from

We a BaddDDD People

Survival
Poems

a poem for my father

how sad it must be
to love so many women
to need so many black
perfumed bodies weeping
underneath you.
                              when i remember all those nights
i filled my mind with
long wars between short
sighted trojans & greeks
while you slapped some
wide hips about in
your pvt dungeon,
when i remember your
deformity   i want to
do something about your
makeshift manhood.
i guess
              that is why
on meeting your sixth
wife, i cross myself
with her confessionals.

blk / rhetoric

for Killebrew Keeby, Icewater, Baker, Gary Adams and Omar Shabazz

who's gonna make all
that beautiful blk / rhetoric
mean something.
                    like
i mean
                who's gonna take
the words
                blk / is / beautiful
and make more of it
than blk / capitalism.
                        u dig?
            i mean
                    like who's gonna
take all the young / long / haired
natural / brothers and sisters
and let them
                grow till
                            all that is
impt is them
            selves
                        moving in straight /
revolutionary / lines
                        toward the enemy
(and we know who that is)
                        like. man.
who's gonna give our young
blk / people new heroes
        (instead of catch / phrases)
        (instead of cad / ill / acs)
        (instead of pimps)

27

(instead of wite / whores)
(instead of drugs)
(instead of new dances)
(instead of chit / ter / lings)
(instead of a 35¢ bottle of ripple)
(instead of quick / fucks in the hall / way
    of wite / america's mind)
like.   this.   is an S O S
    me. calling. . . . .
                        calling. . . . .
                                    some / one
    pleasereplysoon.

personal letter no. 3

nothing will keep
us young you know
not young men or
women who spin
their youth on
cool playing sounds.
we are what we
are what we never
think we are.
no more wild geo
graphies of the
flesh. echoes. that
we move in tune
to slower smells.
it is a hard thing
to admit that
sometimes after midnight
i am tired
of it all.

television / poem

how many of u niggers watched
ted
    kennedy
        on TV yesterday
            while
he sed
    to the motion / picture / capital
       of the world.   (amurica)
   i am still moral
          u know.
i am still that / bright / eyed
    descendant
       of patriotism
i am still running for president
   yo / soon - to - be - / king
    removed from his
     here / di / tary throne
by a mild / republican / battle.
         victory.
how many of u niggers cried
while teddy /
     boy   confessed / talked
bout his
    in / dis / creet   indiscretion.
          & made
u forgive him.
    yeah.   all u blk / jesuses
      how many
niggers have u forgiven so readily?

right on: wite america

1.

it is quite
evident by now
that kennedys
are kill
        able
easily
assassinated
cuz after all
the money and
polish is washed
away in blood
what u got
left cept
poor dirty /
        irish /
            american
(and we know what that
        means in wite america)

right on: wite america

2.

white america is saying
stand up & be counted
as a conservative
                    or die wite/
liberal if u think u
can be our great/
                    wite / president.
and chickens do
come home to roost
cuz
        a / mer / ica /
is now killing her own
after all the
                    terrible / blk / deaths /
of our
        terrible / blk / yrs.

right on: wite america

3.

this country might have
been a pio
            neer land
once.
        but.   there ain't
no mo
          indians   blowing
custer's mind
              with a different
image of america.
                    this country
might have
            needed shoot /
outs / daily /
            once.
                        but there ain't
no mo real / wite /   all american
                        bad/guys.
just.
        u & me.
                blk/ and un/armed.
this country might have
been a pion
            eer land.   once.
                            and it still is.
check out
            the falling
gun/shells   on our blk/ tomorrows.

right on: wite america

4.

for: gun/collection/wk/decreed by Mayor Alioto

HEAR YE!   HEAR YE!

starting july 4th is
bring in yr/guns/down/to/
yr/nearest/po/lice/station
no questions/asked/
                    wk.
and yr/po/lice/dept/
will welcome
all yr/
illegal/guns.   (and they won't say a thing)
            cept maybe
at the next re/bel/lion
maybe just
            the small sound
of murder:
            yr/own . . .

in the courtroom

and they were mostly
all blk/
        daid/dyin people
in the courtroom
           they didn't
know it though.
           i mean even those with
lawyers &
        sure/cases.
           one defendant
confessed his guilt
        of another crime
to avoid this one
        here on stage rite
courtroom no. 6
        and the wite judge
        (fair one i'm told)
sed u've served 11 months & 1 day
that's enuff
        time fo that charge.
           and
the daid/dying/man
        next to me
nods and
        nods
        and nods   away
his life.   till those round him   cough
slight coughs.
        die small deaths
           inhale more smoke.
in the courtroom
        arena of our life.

summer words of a sistuh addict

the first day i shot dope
was on a sunday.
                    i had just come
home from church
                    got mad at my motha
cuz she got mad at me. u dig?
                    went out.   shot up
behind a feelen gainst her.
                              it felt good.
gooder than dooing it. yeah.
                              it was nice.
i did it. uh.huh.   i did it.   uh. huh.
i want   to do it again.   it felt so gooooood.
                    and as the sistuh
                    sits in her silent/
                    remembered/high
                    someone leans for
                    ward gently asks her:
                         sistuh.
                         did u
                         finally
                    learn how to hold yo/mother?
and the music of the day
                    drifts in the room
to mingle with the sistuh's young tears.
                    and we all sing.

on watching a world series game

O say can u see
on the baseball diamond
all the fans
                    clappen for they nigger/players
yeh.
            there ain't nothing like a
            nigger playen in the noon/day
            sun for us fun/loving/spectators.
                                    sometimes
they seem even human.
                        (that is to say
                                every now and then.)
hooray.   hurrah.   hooray.
                            my.   that nigger's
tough on that mound.
                        can't git no
batters past him.
                        wonder where he
was found.
                makes u wonder if
it's still a wite man's game.
                        WHO that flexing
his wite muscles.
                    oh god yes.   another wite hero
to save us from total blk/ness.
                            Carl YASTRZEMSKI
yastruski.   YASTROOSKI.
        ya - fuck - it.   yeh.

                                        it's america's
most famous past time
                                    and the name
        of the game
        ain't baseball.

Love/Songs/Chants

10:15 AM — April 27, 1969
poem

and
     every thing
          that is any
           thing
begins again.
        stops
          to make a left turn
at one / way / streets.
          and the self
               becomes reduced
in time to the nothingness of this
wite / assed / universe
          and down / the / cheek / tears
flow south / ward
        to the womb
            buryen
a wild / nigguh / woman's dreams
in
     bamboo madness.

last poem i'm gonna write bout us

some
times i dream bout
u & me
runnen down
a street laughen.
me no older
u no younger
than we be.
& we finalee catch
each other.
laugh.   tooouch
in the nite.
some
times
i turn a corner
of my mind
& u be there
loooooking
at me.
& smilen.
yo/far/away/smile.
& i moooove
to u.
& the day is not any day.   & yes ter day
is looonNNg

goooNNe.   & we just be.   Some
times i be steady dreamen bout u
cuz i waaannNt

neeeeEEeeD u so

      baaaaAdDD.

with u no younger &

me no older

      than we be.

for our lady

yeh.
      billie.   if someone
had loved u like u
shud have been loved
ain't no tellen what
kinds of songs
           u wud have swung
gainst this country's wite mind.
or what kinds of lyrics
           wud have pushed us from
our blue / nites.
        yeh.   billie.
if some blk / man
        had reallee
made u feel
      permanentlee warm.
ain't no tellen
        where the jazz of yo/songs.
        wud have led us.

TCB/en
Poems

"To Fanon, culture meant only one thing - an environment shaped to help us & our children grow, shaped by ourselves in action against the system that enslaves us."

the cracker is not to be played with.
he is the
enslaver/
            master.   we the slaves
the evillllll he does is not new
cannot be resolved
            thru rhetoric/
            hate/
             poems/
           loooooooven more than one
              wooooooooooman.
the cracker is deep
            deeper than the
400 yrs of our slavery.
we must
watch our
slavery
especially when it looks like freedom.
cuz slaves can look beautiful, talk beautifullee,
can be deceived by the D E V I L
                   who lights our small
flames of rage
           then extinguishes them when
they threaten to spread.
              the master is
mas/ter/ful.

is the SUPREME ANIMAL of
destruction and cannot be destroyed with only:
long dresses - swahili - curses - soul food -
fervor - dashikis - naturrrals - poems -
SOUL - rage - leather jackets - slogans -
polygamy - yoruba.   NO. WE NEED.
                        WAR. DISCIPLINE. LEARNEN.
LAND.   PLANNEN.   LOVE.   AND
                                POWER. POWER. blacker
than the smell of death
                    we the hunters need
to destroy
            the BEAST
        who enslaves us.

why i don't get high on shit

cuz it says
nigger.   u stupid.   u an
ass.   u suicidal.   an
escapist.   i'll help u die
escape.   just take these pills/
weed/
    stuff
      everyday.   & come with
me to tripland.   change colors.
      get wite.   forget
u blk ever been blk
forget that blk/woman
waiten for u
yo/blk/children.   yo/blk/
nation.
    c'mon fooooool.
      suckerrrrr.   take some
more of my shittttt.
    & stay dead.
      forever.

sunday / evening at gwen's

and we came that sun day
etheridge &
                i to that
quiet / looooking / street
                      that held
a blk/
      woman / poet's
   thots
                and we came
that sun
      day   & saw her
naturaaal
          beauty.
              so quiet.   but
full of fire
          when it bees necessary.
& we came that day
              to read our work
but left
      knooowing
            hers.

—a poem for nina simone to put some music to and blow our nigguh / minds—

yeh   yeh. yeh. yeh. yeh.   yeh. yeh. yeh. yeh. yeh.

taught them to wear big naturals
told them they wuz to be blk / & proud
now they bees ready.
                    now they bees ready.
to be mo than pretty and loud.
taught them to dig on themselves
ran down malcolm & garvey too
now they bees ready.
                    now they bees ready.
to be badder than me and you.

taught them new ways of dressing.
wore dashikis and lapas so bright
now they bees ready.
                    now they bees ready.
to take the past and give it some light.

yeh. yeh. yeh yeh. yeh. yeh. yeh. yeh. yeh. yeh.

young brothers / sister, they be something else
concrete actions, not just talk for them
now they bees ready.
                    now they bees ready.
but who's ready for them? huh, huh?
    but who's ready for them?

a ballad for stirling street
(to be sung)

For Amina and Amira Baraka

jest finished readen a book
   bout howard street
guess it had to be written
   bout howard street

now someone shud write one
   bout stirling street
show the beauty of blk / culture
   on stirling street
need to hear bout brothers
   TCB/en on stirling street
need to see sun / wrapped / sisters

   on that black street
need to see Imamu and Amina
   walken blue / indigo / tall
need to hear the loud harambees
   strike gainst the wall

jest finished readen a book bout
   howard street
i've read a whole lot of books like
   howard street
if each one of us moved to a
   howard street
and worked hard like they do on
   stirling street

wudn't be no mo howard sts at all
all the howard sts wud fall - fall - fall
and won't that be good.

                              yeh. yeh.
                              and won't that be good.
                                    yeh.   yeh.   yeh.

now poem.   for us.

don't let them die out
all these old / blk / people
don't let them cop out
with their memories
of slavery / survival.
                    it is our
heritage.
            u know.   part / african.
part / negro.
            part / slave
sit down with em brothas & sistuhs.
                        talk to em.   listen to their
tales of victories / woes / sorrows.
                            listen to their blk /
myths.
        record them talken their ago talk
for our tomorrows.
                    ask them bout the songs of
births.   the herbs
            that cured
                their aches.   the crazy /
                        niggers blowen
                        some cracker's cool.
the laughter
comen out of tears.
let them tell us of their juju years
        so ours will be that much stronger.

3

from

Love Poems

Why

Why must i string my hate
like japanese lanterns
over our pulse?
A minstrel's pain sings
in my thighs
i walk long walks against you
while in my dreams
we are green clay
ripening on canvas.

Poem No. 1

my husband sits
buddha like
watching me weave my
self among the sad
young men of my time.
he thinks i am going
to run away.
maybe i will.

July

the old men and women
quilt their legs
in the shade
while tapestry pigeons
strut their necks.
as i walk, thinking
about you my love,
i wonder what it is
to be old
and swallow death each day
like warm beer.

Father and Daughter

1.

it is difficult to believe that we
ever talked. how did we spend the night
while seasons passed in place of words? Outright
nothing is ever lost; save fantasy
that painted plastic walls with shades and
rolled soft violets while red fruit fell.
along your distant shore i heard you tell
of swollen dawns, and as you crossed the land
of stones you did not turn to sift the
mirror of my sands. This your caress.
in me the wings of owls who gathered flesh
began to turn and gave affinity
to skillful breaths that filled the air
with screaming. Who screams? life is everywhere.

2.

you cannot live here and bend my heart
amid the rhythm of your screams. Apart
still venom sleeps and drains down thru the years
touch not these hands once live with shears
i live a dream about you; each man
alone. You need the sterile woods old age can
bring, no opening of the veins whose smell
will bruise light breasts and burst our shell
of seeds. the landslide of your season
burns the air: this mating has no reason.
don't cry. late grief is not enough. the motion
of your tides still flows within: the ocean
of deep blood that drowns the land. we die:
while young moons rage and wander in the sky.

Haiku

from a husband

At each turn i hear
my child and see women who
resemble my wife.

Poem No. 3

i gather up
each sound
you left behind
and stretch them
on our bed.
                    each nite
i breathe you
and become high.

Poem No. 4

i am here in
my usual place
nothing is turned

on. even i cannot
turn from this
quiet unfolding

my skin. O i am
marked with
this nite's welts

wooing my hands
until they creep
as slowly as a

child's ache, i
touch my pulse.
tell me O pulse

is my breath
out of tune?
i am not a

face of my
own choosing.
still. i am.

i am. and see
my soul elaborate
with furs.

Magic

short magic
is a kiss
in the street
with hangers
on hoping
for more
action.
long magic
is days
wrapped
in your
Black
juice

Words

we were so stricken
by school
and routine
how could we
string our steps.
                    (the days ran in
                            blue shawls)
we moved and
in between we
loved by alphabet.
                    (the nites tucked themselves
                            in, afraid to look)
Now. i at
thirty. You at
thirty-two are
sculptured stains
and my death
comes with
enormous eyes
and my dreams
turn in deformity.

Haiku

we grow up my love
because as yet there is no
other place to go

After the fifth day

with you
i pressed the
rose you brought me
into one of fanon's books.
it has no odor now.
                    but
i see you. handing me a red
rose and i remember
my birth.

Haiku

Was it yesterday
love we shifted the air and
made it blossom Black?

Haiku

O i am so sad, i
go from day to day like an
ordained stutterer.

Prelude to Nothing

i am trying to drain my mind
of all secretions. only then
will i be able to remember
just what it was i said and did
that made you paint your face
until it disappeared
in pale blue noise.
i acknowledge the diseases
of the brain: adolescence.
uncaring minds carrying too
many unexplored chills to hum.
forgetfulness. sadistic brains
that genuflect then chant
no hailmarysfullofgrace
the world is too much with us . . .
i challenge the mind to believe in man
in any man who loves without hating.
What's that you say?
NOW HEAR THIS. NOW HEAR THIS.
man hasn't been invented yet.
i thought not, but what was
that i found snoring
next to
me early one morning?

Blues

in the night
in my half hour
negro dreams
i hear voices knocking at the door
i see walls dripping screams up
and down the halls
                                won't someone open
the door for me? won't some
one schedule my sleep
and don't ask no questions?
noise.
            like when he took me to his
home away from home place
and i died the long sought after
death he'd planned for me.
and two days later
when i was talking
i started to grin.
as everyone knows
i am still grinning.

Kaleidoscope

tumbling blue and brown
tulips that leap
into frogs
women dancing in metal
blue raindrops sliding
into green diamonds
turtles crawling outward
into stars
electric w's
spreading beyond words
papooses turning
into hearts
and butterflies stretching
into court jesters
who jump
amid red splinters
just like you . . .

Haiku

o i was wide and
open unto him and he
moved in me like rain

Ballad

(after the spanish)

forgive me if i laugh
you are so sure of love
you are so young
and i too old to learn of love.

the rain exploding
in the air is love
the grass excreting her
green wax is love
and stones remembering
past steps is love,
but you. You are too young
for love
and i too old.

Once. What does it matter
When or who, i knew
of love.
i fixed my body
under his and went
to sleep in love
all trace of me
was wiped away

forgive me if i smile
Young heiress of a naked dream
You are so young
and i too old to learn of love.

Poem No. 7

when he came home
from her
he poured me on
the bed and slid
into me like glass.
and there was
the sound of splinters

Sequences

1.
today I am
tired of sabbaths.
I seek a river of sticks
scratching the spine.
O I have laughed the clown's air
now my breath dries in paint.

2.
what is this profusion?
the sun does not burn
a cure, but hoards
while I stretch upward.
I hear, turning
in my shrug
a blaze of horns.
O I had forgotten parades
belabored with dreams.

3.
in my father's time
I fished in ponds
without fishes.
arching my throat,
I gargled amid nerves
and sang of redeemers.

      (o where have you been sweet
        redeemer, sharp redeemer,
     o where have you been baroque
      shimmer?

i have been in coventry
where ghosts danced in my veins
i have heard you in all refrains.)

4.
ah the lull of
a yellow voice
that does not whine
with roots.
I have touched breasts
and buildings answered.
I have breathed
moth-shaped men
without seeds.
(O indiscriminate sleeves)

(once upon an afternoon
i became still-life
i carried a balloon
and a long black knife.)

5.
love comes with pink eyes
with movements that run
green then blue again.
my thighs burn in crystal.

Old Words

We are the dead
ones the slow
fast suicides
of our time.
we are the dis
enfranchised ones
the buyers of bread
one day removed
from mold
we are maimed
in our posture

1. did you hear me start
    my herding song that
                summer nite?
    it is autumn
    now and the nite
    multiplies by threes.
    can you hear me poet?
                one sound was you
    And as i sang you
    blue masks marched
    from your face
                holy with stains.
    O mass produced faces
    i have burned myself out
    now my ashes have
    no place to lean.

sing it billie
                baby.
sing away that ill wind
blowing you no good.
        no good.
ill wind.
                spread yo/strange
fruit amid these
stones. we all
strangers here. sing.
        i hear
yo/words quivering with silks
        i smell
your black soul.
        sweet.

2. it is horrible to be.
   gigantic fornicators advance
   toward me shrieking
   maternity cries.
   and as i run i
   trip over my deformity.
   this is a fool's world
   pain is an idiot's ailment
   for the wise man knows
   how to reconnoiter pain
   and make it colloquial.

                    go Prez. go man. move
        those plastic hands
        up and down that sax
        blow. man. blow. ride
        yo/saxophone cross
        the stage and back again
        we all riders
        here. blow.
                    man.
        can't you see this
        transfixed audience
        staring at you while
        you bleed.
                    blow.
                            ride.
        bleed . . . blow.

3. Are we ever what we should be?
    seated in our circle of agonies
    we do not try to tune our breaths
    since we cannot sing together
    since we cannot waltz our eyes
    since we cannot love.
    since we have wooed this world
    too long with separate arias of revolution
    mysticism hatred and submission
    since we have rehearsed our
    deaths apart. Now. let us abandon
    past heresies. now.

when small men stretch for greatness
via wars on poverty,
(in the 20th century at a time of Punitive
     Contaminated
Repressive Wars)
when men disfigure their bodies
to become holy in space and walk
without footsteps;
(in the 20th century at a time of
grinning Life – Copyrighted – Astronauts)
when men stuff their mouths with
murderous soliloquies and urinate
on hungry faces;
(in the 20th century at a time of
illiterate adulterous industrious hungers)

>   we have come to
>   believe that we are
>   not. to be we
>   must be loved or
>   touched and proved
>   to be. this earth
>   turns old
>   and rivers grow lunatic
>   with rain. how i wish
>   i could lean in your cave
>   and creak with the winds.

Haiku

if i had known, if
i had known you, i would have
left my love at home.

To You/Who Almost Turned/Me On

yeah.
>   my man.
> got no place else
> to go. have to turn
> to myself.
>   child/like
> am i my man.
> i believe in fairy tales
> (tales told by fairy men)
>   slow
>   fabricated
>   stories that scare.
> like. today.
>   full
> of yesterday's hide and
> seek shadows, i kissed
> a strange mouth out of
> control. but.
>   strangers are
> rainbow colored and
>   i am
> color blind.

Formula

to live
believe
in no
one
never touch
for each
gentle face
you would
caress
is death.
know that
nothing
ripens
all is
maimed
and obscene
with eyes.
remember
life is one
long
breath
forever
out of tune.

Haiku

there are things sadder
than you and I. some people
do not even touch.

Poem No. 8

i've been a woman
    with my legs stretched by the wind
      rushing the day
        thinking i heard your voice
          while it was only the nite
        moving over
           making room for the dawn.

Poem No. 10

you keep saying you were always there
waiting for me to see you.
                    you said that once
on the wings of a pale green butterfly
you rode across san francisco's hills
and touched my hair as i caressed
a child called militancy
you keep saying you were always there

holding my small hand
              as i walked
unbending indiana streets i could not see around
and you grew a black mountain
of curves and i turned
and became soft again
you keep saying you were always there

repeating my name softly
              as i slept in
slow pittsburgh blues and you made me
sweat nite dreams that danced
and danced until the morning
rained yo / red delirium
You keep saying you were always there
You keep saying you were always there
           Will you stay love
          Now that i am here?

Welcome home. my prince

welcome home. my prince
into my white season of no you
welcome home
      to my songs
that touch yo / head
          and rain green laughter
          in greeting
welcome home
to this monday
      that has grown up
with the sound of yo / name
for i have chanted to yesterday's sun
to hurry back with
his belly full of morning
          and you have
come
    and i cannot look up at you.
          my body
trembles and i mumble things as you
stand tall and sacred
so easily in yo / self
          but i am here
to love you
      to carry yo / name on my
ankles like bells
      to dance in
    Yo/ arena of love.
    You are tattooed on the round/soft/
    parts of me.
      And yo/ smell is
    Always with me.

Haiku

your love was a port
of call where many ships docked
until morning came.

Haiku

i could love you Black
man if you'd let me walk in
side you and become you.

I Have Walked a Long Time

i have walked a long time
much longer than death that splinters
wid her innuendos.
my life, ah my alien life,
is like an echo of nostalgia
bringen blue screens to bury clouds
rinsen wite stones stretched among the sea.

     you, man, will you remember me when i die?
     will you stare and stain my death and say
     i saw her dancen among swallows
     far from the world's obscenities?
     you, man, will you remember and cry?

and i have not loved.
always
while the body prowls
the soul catalogues each step;
while the unconscious unbridles feasts
the flesh knots toward the shore.
ah, i have not loved
wid legs stretched like stalks against sheets
wid stomachs drainen the piracy of oceans
wid mouths discarden the gelatin
to shake the sharp self.

i have walked by memory of others
between the blood night
and twilights

i have lived in tunnels
and fed the bloodless fish;
between the yellow rain
and ash,
i have heard the rattle
of my seed.
so time, like some pearl necklace embracen
a superior whore, converges
and the swift spider binds my breast.

you, man, will you remember me when i die?
will you stare and stain my death and say
i saw her applauden suns
far from the grandiose audience?
you, man, will you remember and cry?

Hey There

three yr old sistuh
going on forty
you something else
with yo/wite/teeth/smile
that be sayin
            i love you.

A Blk/Woman/Speaks

i am deep/blk/soil
they have tried to pollute me
with a poison called America.
they have tried to
                        scorch my roots
with dope
            they have tried to
drown my dreams with alcohol
with too many men who spit
their foam on top of my fruit
till it drops
                rotten in America's
parks.
        but i am deeeeeEEEp
blue/blk/soil
                and you can hear the
sound of my walken
as i bring forth green songs
from a seasoned breast
as i burn on our evening bed
of revolution.
                i, being blk
                    woooOOOMAN
know only the way of the womb
for i am deep/red/soil
            for our emergen Blk Nation.

Poem No. 12

When i am woman, then i shall be wife of your eyes

When i am woman, then i shall receive the sun

When i am woman, then i shall be shy with pain

When i am woman, then shall my laughter stop the wind

When i am woman, then i shall swallow the earth

When i am woman, then i shall give birth to myself

When i am woman, ay-y-y, ay-y-y, ay-y-y,

When i am woman . . .

Haiku (written from Peking)

let me wear the day
well so when it reaches you
you will enjoy it.

Depression

1.
I have gone into my eyes
bumping against sockets that sing
smelling the evening from under the sun
where the waterless bones move
toward their rivers in incense
a piece of light crawls up and down
then turns a corner.

As when drunken air molts in beds,
tumbling over blankets that cover sweat
nudging into sheets continuing dreams;
so I have settled in wheelbarrows
grotesque with wounds,
small and insistent as sleigh bells.

Am i a voice delighting in the sand?
Look how the masks rock on the winds
moving in tune to leaves.
i shed my clothes.
am I a seed consumed by breasts
without the weasel's eye
or the spaniel teeth of a child?

2.
I have cried all night
tears pouring out of my forehead
sluggish in pulse,

tears from a spinal soul

that run in silence to my birth

Ayyyy! am I born? I cannot peel the flesh.

I hear the moon daring

to dance these rooms.

O to become a star.

stars seek their own mercy

and sigh the quiet, like gods.

Listening to Jimmy Garrison
(Pittsburgh, Pa.)

Who you be remembering
lil
jimmy garrison?
                        do you be hearing
Coltrane creaking with the wind
while your music spills our birth?
                        What
you be crying sweet / playing / jimmy
as your hands caress those strings
until we drop all secret smells.
hey.   hey yyy.   hey yyyyy
                        jimmy garrison maaan
What you be thinking
                        on this pittsburgh nite
Where pain swears above the city
and we lean back.
                        and listen.
                        and remember.
forget you.
                        and remember.
                        smile at you
and remember.
                        and looooove . . . . . .

Haiku

in your wet season
i painted violets and
drank their deep channels.

Haiku

O this day like an
orange peeled against the sky
murmurs me and you.

Poem No. 15

Is it possible to love so much?
On this day, full of children who sing,
i love that man passing in exile
i love his eyes pilgrim with echoes.
On this day, full of children soon to learn,
i love his dawns that smell of shuttered blood
i love his moist limbs framed in fever.
On this day full of consumptive smells,
I love.

4

from

A Blues Book
for Blue Black
Magical Women

Past

COME into Black geography
you, seated like Manzu's cardinal,
come up through tongues
multiplying memories
and to avoid descent
among wounds
cruising like ships,
climb into these sockets
golden with brine.

                              because i was born
                              musicians to two
                              black braids, i
                              cut a blue
                              song for america.
                              and you, cushioned
                              by middleclass springs,
                              saw ghettos
                              that stretched
                              voices into dust
                              turned corners
                              where people walked
                              on their faces.
                              i sang unbending
                              songs and gathered gods
                              convenient as christ.

i am the frozen
face, here my
face marches
toward new myths
while spring runs
green with ghosts.
i am the living
mask, here my
skin worn
with adolescence
peels like
picasso's planes
and the earth
in one fold of
permanence stares
at the skies

if i had a big piece of dust
to ride on, i would gather up my pulse
and follow disposable dreams
and all things being equal
they would pass into butterflies
& quiver in sprawling yellow.

1. woman

COME ride my birth, earth mother
tell me how i have become, became
this woman with razor blades between
her teeth.
              sing me my history O earth mother
about tongues multiplying memories
about breaths contained in straw.
pull me from the throat of mankind
where worms eat, O earth mother.
come to this Black woman. you.
rider of earth pilgrimages.
tell me how i have held five bodies
in one large cocktail of love
and still have the thirst of beginning sip.
tell me. tellLLLLLL me. earth mother
for i want to rediscover me. the secret of me
the river of me. the morning ease of me.
i want my body to carry my words like aqueducts.
i want to make the world my diary
and speak rivers.

rise up earth mother
out of rope-strung-trees
dancing a windless dance
come phantom mother
dance me a breakfast of births
let your mouth spill me forth
so i creak with your mornings.
come old mother, light up my mind
with a story bright as the sun.

2. earth mother

(low singing is heard)

old/   *Bells. bells. bells.*

woman's/   *let the bells ring.*

voice/   *BELLS. BELLS. BELLS*

ring the bells to announce

this your earth mother.

for the day is turning

in my thighs And you are born

BLACK GIRL.

come, i am calling to you.

this old earth mother of the elaborate dreams

come. come nearer. girl. *NEARER.*

i can almost see your face now.

COME CLOSER.

Low/   yes. there you are. i have stuffed

laugh/   your whole history in my mouth

i. your earth mother

was that hungry once. for knowledge.

come closer. ah little Black girl

i see you.

i can see you coming

towards me little girl

running from seven to thirty-five

in one day.

i can see you coming

girl made of black braids

i can see you coming

in the arena of youth

girl shaking your butt to double dutch days
i can see you coming
girl racing dawns
i can see you coming
girl made of black rain
i can see you coming.

3. young/black/girl

Fivetenfifteentwenty
twentyfivethirtythirtyfiveforty
fortyfivefiftyfiftyfivesixty
sixtyfiveseventy
seventyfiveeighty
eightyfiveninety
ninetyfiveonehundredreadyornothere i come
REAdyornothereicome!
one
two
three. i see you.
                    and you. and YOU. AND YOU.

AND YOU U U U U U U—step/mother.
woman of my father's youth
who stands at a mirror
elaborate with smells
all shiny like my new copper penny.
telling me through a parade of smiles
you are to be my new mother. and your painted lips
outlined against time become time
and i look on time and hear you
who threw me in angry afternoon closets
til i slipped beneath the cracks
like light. and time stopped.
and i turned into myself
a young girl breathing in crusts
and listened to those calling me.

to/	*no matter what they do*
be/	*they won't find me*
chanted/	*no matter what they say*
	i won't come out.

i have hidden myself behind black braids
and stutters and cannot be seen.

to/	*no matter what they do*
be/	*they won't find me*
chanted/	*no matter what they say*
	i won't come out.

i listen to words asking
what did she say?
why can't she talk normal talk?
there's something wrong with that one!
she got the demon inside of her or something!
strange one!!
too quiet!!!

to/	*no matter what they do*
be/	*they won't find me*
chanted/	*no matter what they say*
	i won't come out . . .

Coming out from alabama
to the island city of corner store jews
patting bigbuttedblack women in tune
to girlie can i help ya?

girlie what you want today?
a good sale on pork today.
girlie.
        girlie.
            girlie.

coming out from alabama
to the island city of perpetual adolescence
where i drink my young breasts
and stay thirsty
always hungry for more than the
georgewashingtonhighschoolhuntercollegedays
of america.
            remember parties
        where we'd grindddDDDD
        and grindddDDDDD
        but not too close
        cuz if you gave it up
        everybody would know. and tell.
        and grindddding was enough. the closeness
        of bodies in project basement
        recreation rooms was enough
        to satisfy the platter's sounds
        spinning you into body after body
        then walking across the room
        where young girls watched each other
        like black vultures
        pretending nothing had happened
        leaving young brothers in conditions
        they satisfied with out of the
        neighborhood girls . . .

Coming out from alabama
into smells i could not smell
into nites that corner lights
lit dimly.

i walked into young
womanhood. Could not hear
my footsteps in the streets
could not hear the rhythm of
young Black womanhood.

4. young womanhood

And i entered into young
  womanhood. you asked.
  who goes there?

who calls out
  to this perennial
  Black man of ruin?

and time on her annual
  pilgrimage squatted and
  watched as i called
  out to love from my door.

what a lovely smell love
was. like a stream of
violets that warmed your face.

and i was found at the four
  corners of love. a Black
  man and I imprisoned
  with laughter at himself.

a man made sterile
by hatred
a famine man
starved and starving
those around him
in this plentiful country.

as i entered into my
young womanhood i became
   a budding of laughter. i
   moved in liquid dreams
   wrapped myself in a
   furious circuit of love
   gave out quick words
   and violent tremblings
   and kisses that bit
   and drew blood
   and the seasons fell
   like waterfalls on my thighs

and i dressed myself
in foreign words
   became a proper painted
   european Black faced american
   going to theatre parties and bars
   and cocktail parties and bars
   and downtown village apartments
   and bars and ate good cheese
   and caviar with wine that
   made my stomach stretch for artificial warmth.

   danced with white friends who
   included me because that was
   the nice thing to do in the late
   fifties and early sixties

and i lost myself
down roads
i had never walked.

and my name was
without honor
and i became a
stranger at my birthright.

~

who is that
making noise on this earth
while good people sleep
i wondered, as i turned
in our three year old bed of love.

in the morning
i reminded you of the noise
and you said,
just some niggers pretending
to be the wind.

the nite brought more noise
   like a swift courier
   and i leaped from our bed
   and followed the sound.

   and visions came from the wall.
   bodies without heads, laughter without mouths.
   then faces crawling on the walls
   like giant spiders,
   came toward me
   and my legs buckled and
       i cried out.

one face touched mine and said:

   "you are a singer of songs
      but you do not listen to what men have said
      therefore you cannot sing."

a second face murmured:

   "you are a reader of books
      but books that do not teach you truth
      are false messiahs."

a third face smiled as i closed my eyes:

   "you move as a free woman,
      but your body is a monument to slavery
      and is dead."

When morning came
you took me to one
inebriated with freud.

massaging his palms
he called out to me
a child of the south,
and i listened to
european words
that rushed out to
me and handcuffed
me.

And for a while i rode
on horseback
among my youth

remembered southern days
and nites
remembered a beginning new york
girlhood where tall buildings looked
like aqueducts.
remembered stutters
i could not silence.

at the end of a month
when he couldn't explain
away continued acts that
killed.
at the end of a month
of stumbling alibis,
after my ancestral voices
called out to me against

past and future murders,
i moved away from reconciling myself to
murderers
and gave myself up to
the temper of the times.

stood against discrimination
in housing.
jobs.
picketed. sat in. sang about
overcoming that which would
never come.
closed woolworths. marched
against T.V. stations while
ducking horseriding cops
advancing like funeral hawks.

was knocked to the ground
while my child screamed
at the cannibals on horseback.

and i screeeamed.
calling out to those who
would listen.

called out from carolinian
slave markets, mississippi
schools, harlem streets that
beasts populated us.
beasts with no human heartbeats
when they came among BLACKNESS.

and i vomited up the past.
the frivolous years and i
threw up the smiles and bowings
and nods that had made
me smile so many smiles.

and i vomited up the stench
of the good ship *Jesus*
sailing to the new world
with Black gold
i vomited up the cries of
newborn babies thrown
overboard

i vomited up the waters
that had separated me
from Dahomey and Arabia
and Timbuktu and Muhammad
and Asia and Allah.

i vomited up denmark vesey
and nat turner and rebellious
slave women
their big stomachs split open
in the sun.

i vomited up white robed choirs
and preachers hawking their sermons
to an unseeing God.

and i vomited out names like beasts.
and death. and pigs and death.
and devil and death
and the vomiting ceased.
and i was alone.

      ~

woke up alone
to the middle sixties
full of the rising wind of history

alive in a country of echoes
convulsive with gods
alone with the
apocalypse of beasts,
in america. The repository
of european promise.
rabid america.
   where death is
   gay and obscene
   and legal in the sight
   of an unseeing God.

5. womanhood

Moving. constantly.
some destiny calling
out to me
to explore the sea
and the sky.
to talk against
sleeping on our knees.

and i moved.
eldest daughter of the womb.
eldest daughter of the world.

open to all Blackness
making the country keep in step
to these our new sounds.
to the music of a
million Black souls.

and i called out to prophesy
to make me a woman
of the beginning tribe
to make me a woman of
tyrannical love to
cover our wounds.

and
Blackness was the
order of the day.
all who looked were
enchanted and
chanted who they once were

and we fell down upon
the earth and became ourselves.

and
Blackness was the
order of the day
    and the voice of Elijah was
    heard opening the
    door of the world
    and all who came
    after him,
    poets and soothsayers
    rappers and raconteurs
    politicians and activists,
    writers and teachers,
    sang his wisdom.
    and we fell down
    upon the earth and
    became ourselves.

and
i gave birth to myself,
twice. in one hour.
i became like Maat,
unalterable in my
love of Black self and
righteousness.
and i heard the
trumpets of a new age
and i fell down
upon the earth
and became myself.

Present

1

THIS woman vomiting her
hunger over the world
this melancholy woman forgotten
before memory came
this yellow movement bursting forth like
coltrane's melodies all mouth
buttocks moving like palm trees,
this honeycoatedalabamianwoman
raining rhythms of blue/black/smiles
this yellow woman carrying beneath her breasts
pleasures without tongues
this woman whose body weaves
desert patterns,
this woman, wet with wandering,
reviving the beauty of forests and winds
is telling you secrets
gather up your odors and listen
as she sings the mold from memory.

                        there is no place
for a soft/black/woman.
there is no smile green enough or
summertime words warm enough to allow my growth.
and in my head
i see my history
standing like a shy child
and i chant lullabies
as i ride my past on horseback
tasting the thirst of yesterday tribes

hearing the ancient/black/woman
me, singing   hay-hay-hay-hay-ya-ya-ya
                     hay-hay-hay-hay-ya-ya-ya.
like a slow scent
beneath the sun
                and i dance my
creation and my grandmothers gathering
from my bones like great wooden birds
spread their wings
while their long/legged/laughter
stretches the night.
                     and i taste the
seasons of my birth. mangoes. papayas.
drink my woman/coconut/milks
stalk the ancient grandfathers
sipping on proud afternoons
walk with a song round my waist
tremble like a new/born/child troubled
with new breaths
                and my singing
becomes the only sound of a
blue/black/magical/woman. walking.
womb ripe. walking. loud with mornings. walking.
making pilgrimage to herself. walking.

Rebirth

WHEN i stepped off the plane i knew i was home
had been here before. had been away
roaming the cold climate of my mind where
winter and summer hold the same temperature
of need.

and i held up my hands. face. cut by the northern
winds and blood oozed forth kissed the place
of my birth and the sun and sea gather round
my offering and we were one as night is surely day
when you truly understand the need one has for the other.

a green smell rigid as morning
stretched like a young maiden 'cross the land
and i tasting a new geography took off my shoes
let my feet grow in the green dance of growth
and the dance was new and my thighs
burning like chords
left a trail for others to follow when
they returned home as all must surely do to make
past future tense.

the faces smiling at me, the sun drenched faces
like soft leather. they knew that i finally knew
and our eyes met. promised meetings. no words
were spoken for the speech of recognition had been
spoken and the constant movement to your place
of birth where the warm/blue/green seas cradle
your blackness.

the ritual beat of the sun and sea
made my body smile.

creases of laughter covered me
when i saw the sea. & the sea was shocked
by the roar of my laughter coming from my
bowels like some giant wave.
my pores sweated, expelled all past rhythms
brought the chants of one made tall
by the wisdom of suns.
i grew as i rowed out from boulevards
balancing my veins on sails
i grew as the clouds moving 'gainst chills
tilted my flesh till it flaked.
and i sang

> arch me softly
> O summery winds, i am
> strict as the sun.
> rock me O pulse
> i knock all over.
> sing. sing. sing. you
> sister waves. i shall paint
> his silence with seeds.

i remembered the first time i made love
in a room on seventh avenue
on a street of forgotten tribal life
and as the sea entered my pores and
made me stretch and open to be filled
i remember a nite we stretched our
bodies and poured our juices into each other.
it was summer and you called me little one

for my body filled only a small part
of your need.

some faces gathered at the shore.
called out warnings as i walked further
from the land. some faces screamed
no one can grow as tall as the sea. but
i continued to grow and the sea and i greeted
each other with laughter.
each day she measured my growth and said one day
you'll be taller than i.
i cannot remember the color of day
when i had to bend to be caressed by her touch.

whatever is truth becomes known. nine
months passed touching a bottomless sea.
nine months i wandered amid waves
that washed away thirty years of denial.
nine months without stains

nine months passed and my body
heavy with the knowledge of gods
turned landward. came to rest.

wherefore a woman has many fathers,
i keep dreaming of my birth
of two hands moving against chills
tilting the flesh till it flaked.
i became mother of sun. moon. star children.
and the hour of after birth when i turned
into my breath you came and i proclaimed
you without sound.

you. you. Black Man. standing straight
as a sentry. staring in monotony.
LOOK. a savior moves in these breasts,
i who have waltzed the sea hear my
seed running toward your seasons.
you. you. Black redeemer star.
sweeten your points.
i need old silver for my veins.

5

from

It's a New Day
poems for young brothas and sistuhs

For Morani/Mungu/Meusi

As-Salaam-Alaikum my black princes
the morning awaits u.
           the world
awaits yo/young/blackness
sun/children
           of our tomorrow.
Here is my hand
           black/warriors of
our dreams.
           it is soft as the
blue/nite that covered yo/
blackness
           till day began its
morning talk.
           it is hard as
the strength u gather from
yo/father's words pouren
from his mouth like thunder
over a dry land.
           but i am
here to love u my princes.
           to gather
up yo/insides
           and make them
smile dreams.
           for u my loves
will be the doers.
           and yo/deeds
will run red with ancient songs

that play a continuous chant of
it's a new day.

         it's a new new new day
    It's A NEW DAY!

As-Salaam-Alaikum
  young princes.
        the world
awaits yo/young/blackness

Words for Kali and Poochie

Blow our country a life color
you the children of jazz.
Roberta Flack yo/way
in and out of sermons
for soon you begin
          the Black Rhythm of Life
wailing past
   America's supermarket civilization.
go on now.
     sing us yo/riffs that will change the
direction of planets
        you baaaddDD/young/rhythms.
we hear you
      smile a new season
       and Bless The Day We Found You.

Words for Geoffrey and Stephanie Hamilton

History has made this time for you.
that the final result be you
lyrical children of non-poetic times
is not the point.

                 you are. we have
thought you to be. and you come
lighting our underground minds

                                disturbing the trash
of cavish nine to five lives.
you are our poems
a cascading sound of rhyme and meter.
and when you enter into the streets and
walk yo earthquake walks
we live.

City Songs

dope pushers dope pushers
  git outa our parks
  we come to slide on slides
  climb the monkey bars

don't need yo/dope
  to make us git high
  the swings will take us
  way up in the sky.

dope pushers dope pushers
  u ain't no friend
  no matter how you smile
  and always pretend

cuz we know nowadays
  black is a baaddDD groove
  and dope is a trick bag
  for fools fools fools

dope pushers dope pushers
  offa our street
  cuz one of these days
  you gonna meet

some together black men
  who'll show you the score
  and you won't be standing round
  tempting us no mo

dope pushers dope pushers
   change while you can
   it's nation/builden/time
   for black people in every land

so c'mon. c'mon. brothas
   run fas as u can
   and be what u must be
   sun people in a black land.

dope pushers dope pushers
   git back, git back
   cuz to git ahead today
   you gots to be black. black. black.

to P.J. (2 yrs old who sed write a poem for me in Portland, Oregon)

if i cud ever write a
poem as beautiful as u,
little 2/yr/old/brotha,
i wud laugh, jump, leap
up and touch the stars
cuz u be the poem i try for
each time i pick up a pen and paper.
u. and Morani and Mungu
be our blue/blk/stars that
will shine on our lives and
make us finally BE.
if i cud ever write a poem as beautiful
as u, little 2/yr/old/brotha,
poetry wud go out of bizness.

When we come

When we come
riden our green horses
against the tenement dust,
when we come, tall as waves,
holden our black/brown/
high yellow/tomorrows,
then you will hear young hooves
thunderen in space
and we will rise with
rainbows from the sea
to silence
our yesterday blues

when we come
riden our green breath
against the morning sky.

We Can Be

we can be anything we want
for we are the young ones
walken without footprints
moven our bodies in tune
to songs
      echoen us. the beautiful
black ones.
      recently born.
            walken new
            rhythms
leaven behind us a tap dancer's dream
of sunday nite ed sullivan shows.
WE WILL BE
      ALL that we want
for we are the young ones
bringen the world to a Black Beginnen.

from

I've Been a Woman

(Haikus / Tankas & Other Love Syllables)

i have looked into
    my father's eyes and seen an
    african sunset.

    i paraplegic
in madness came to you. you
    cauterized me home.

don't go. if you go
    i won't hear me. morning will
    walk from me with life.

(for gwen brooks)
    woman. whose color
    of life is like the sun, whose
    laughter is prayer.

man, i am trying
    to love you fully in such
    a way so when you
    run the wind from yo/legs leap
    out and kiss my opening thighs.

his voice used to sing
    when he talked to me used to
    smile rivers. and i
    would slide on eyes with him down
    his morning breakfast of sails.

baby. you are sweet
    as watermelon juice run/
    ning down my wide lips.

let me be your flute
    fashioning laughter from this
    bamboo wilderness.

i am settling down
    on you where we are both soft
    and taste like butter.

away from you these
    sheets are mummy tapes i twist
    and turn myself in.

You have stamped your hour
    on me, tattooed yourself on
    me like sheets of silk.

my body waiting
    for the sound of yo / hands is loud
    as a prairie song

at the center of
    me, you, holyman walking
    in lightning colors.

short poem for us slick ones —

the

arabs

ain't got no/

thing on

our oil.

never may my thirst
    for freedom be appeased by
    modern urinals.

the trees are laughing
    at us. positioning their
    leaves in morning smiles.

these autumn trees sit
    cruel as we pretend to eat
    this morning goodbye.

i'm in the middle
       of your thighs squeezing us from
       ancient palaces.

you are amble and
       amiable artist. you
       are my universe.

familiarize your
       self with strength. hold each other
       up against silence.

these words stained with red
       twirl on my tongue like autumn
       rainbows from the sea.

would you please return
       my pulse? i need to tap my
       breathing once again.

before i travel
    to you i raise my sun cup
    in ceremony.

just the two of us
    suspended in each other
    like red morning rain.

morning snow falling
    astride this carousel called
    life. i am sailing.

night pumping like an
    otis redding riff over
    these regimented rooms.

when you left i ran
    through the house in rage banging
    my head against doors.

our bodies made rain

this morning as you pumped from

this stampeding well.

shedding my years and
    earthbound now. midnite trees are
    more to my liking.

        i wish it were mid/
            night again. your legs walking
            us from palaces.

woman. rocking her
    white hair in soft mountain plaits
    feet flat like white tiles.

        like bigger thomas
            i didn't want to love but what
            i loved for. i am.

rocking her white feet
eyes cataracted on youth
she cackles down the
morning masquerading as
her face. i pass in review.

we be. gonna be
even after being. black
mass has always been.

cause we are carving
our silhouettes on the
hips of yesterday
women parading children
in tongues of manhood.

bear the rhythm of
your name and mine wide on green
rivers of change.

how can you comfort
        me? i need the caress of
        centuries. the taste
        of ancestors riding their
        legs in civilization.

what is it about
        me that i claim all the wrong
        lives, the same endings?

        (for sarah fabio)

        a woman who made

        me look down the corridors

        of our black birth.

i guess. this is what
        i want from you. a promise
        made me that no one
        be allowed in the space that
        i have occupied with you.

when i return home
　　　to sleep the shadow of you
　　　covers me with day.

and the joy. feeling
　　　you pressed on me. eyes smiling
　　　over miles and time.

　　　just you. just me. just
　　　　　us. blessed and strong. Moving
　　　　　beside each other.

love. you are. you are
　　　love. i am in, we are in
　　　love. you are. we are.

　　　we are gatherers
　　　　　of bamboo songs that pass be
　　　　　tween us in softness.

earth eyes. breathing me.
defying generations.
earth eyes. loving me.

once i was chaste with
innocence with the walk of
a child unveiled.

you do not know the
high prayer of pain. these screams
hoist my terror up
amid chandelier walls where
i dance my minstrel stutters.

the rain tastes lovely
like yo/sweat draping my body
after lovemaking.

summer has sped a/
    cross this philadelphia land/
    scape warrior style.

who are you/ iden./
    tify yourself. tell me your
    worth amid women.

seventy-one years
    have gathered like mildew on
    her tenement eyes.

when i look at you
    yo/smile becomes a full moon
    waiting for werewolves.

i listen for yo/
    sounds prepare my nostrils for
    yo/smell that has detoured.

what do i know of
    you? you smile little round moon
    smiles from square corners.

missing you is like
    spring standing still on a hill
    amid winter snow.

you have pierced me so
    deeply i cannot turn a
    round without bleeding.

we stumbled into
    each other's lives like two young
    children playing house.

there are times that the
    smell of you, your loud touch makes
    me bend down in pain.

i lean back and feel
     the warmth of you traveling
     from one space to a/
     nother. and iam gone. home/
     bound to where you also live.

i am on top of
     you riding you thru waves hold/
   ing tight to your foam
    spilling juice from my cup
as you pump for my black gold.

from Under a Soprano Sky

Beginnings

Under a Soprano Sky

1.

once i lived on pillars in a green house
boarded by lilacs that rocked voices into weeds.
i bled an owl's blood
shredding the grass until i
rocked in a choir of worms.
obscene with hands, i wooed the world
with thumbs
                    while yo-yos hummed.
was it an unborn lacquer i peeled?
the woods, tall as waves, sang in mixed
tongues that loosened the scalp
and my bones wrapped in white dust
returned to echo in my thighs.

i heard a pulse wandering somewhere
on vague embankments.
O are my hands breathing? I cannot smell the nerves.
i saw the sun
ripening green stones for fields.
O have my eyes run down? i cannot taste my birth.

2.

now as i move, mouth quivering with silks
my skin runs soft with eyes.
descending into my legs, i follow obscure birds
purchasing orthopedic wings.
the air is late this summer.

i peel the spine and flood
the earth with adolescence.
O who will pump these breasts? I cannot waltz my tongue.

under a soprano sky, a woman sings,
lovely as chandeliers.

(section 1)

A poem for my brother
(reflections on his death from AIDS: June 8, 1981)

1 . death

The day you died
a fever starched my bones.
within the slurred
sheets, i hoarded my legs
while you rowed out among the boulevards
balancing your veins on sails.
easy the eye of hunger
as i peeled the sharp
sweat and swallowed wholesale molds.

2 . recovery (a)

What comes after
is consciousness of the morning
of the licensed sun that subdues
immoderate elements.
there is a kindness in illness
the indulgence of discrepancies.

reduced to the ménage of houses
and green drapes that puff their seasons
toward the face.
i wonder what to do now.
i am afraid
i remember a childhood that cried
after extinguished lights
when only the coated banners answered.

3. recovery (b)

There is a savior in these buds
look how the phallic stems distend
in welcome.
O copper flowerheads
confine my womb that i may dwell within.
i see these gardens, whom i love
i feel the sky's sweat on my face
now that these robes no longer bark
i praise abandonment.

4. wake

i have not come for summary.
must i renounce all babylons?
here, without psalms,
these leaves grow white
and burn the bones with dance.
here, without surfs,
young panicles bloom on the clouds and fly
while myths tick grey as thunder.

5. burial

you in the crow's rain
rusting amid ribs
my mouth spills your birth
i have named you prince of boards
stretching with the tides.

you in the toad's tongue
peeling on nerves
look. look. the earth is running palms.

6. (on) (the) (road). again.
somewhere a flower walks in mass
purchasing wholesale christs
sealing white-willow sacraments.

naked on steeples
where trappist idioms sail
an atom peels the air.

O i will gather my pulse
muffled by sibilants
and follow disposable dreams.

elegy

for MOVE* and Philadelphia

1.
philadelphia
    a disguised southern city
squatting in the eastern pass of
colleges cathedrals and cowboys.
philadelphia. a phalanx of parsons
and auctioneers
    modern gladiators
erasing the delirium of death from their shields
while houses burn out of control.

2.
c'mon girl hurry on down to osage st
they're roasting in the fire
smell the dreadlocks and blk/skins
roasting in the fire.

c'mon newsmen and tvmen
hurryondown to osage st and
when you have chloroformed the city
and after you have stitched up your words
hurry on downtown for sanctuary
in taverns and corporations

and the blood is not yet dry.

---

*MOVE: a Philadelphia-based back-to-nature group whose headquarters
was bombed by the police on May 13, 1985, killing men, women, and children.
An entire city block was destroyed by fire.

3.

how does one scream in thunder?

4.

they are combing the morning for shadows
and screams tongue-tied without faces
look. over there. one eye
escaping from its skin
and our heartbeats slowdown to a drawl
and the kingfisher calls out from his downtown capital
And the pinstriped general reenlists
his tongue for combat
and the police come like twin seasons of drought and flood.
they're combing the city for lifeliberty and
the pursuit of happiness.

5.

how does one city scream in thunder?

6.

hide us O lord
deliver us from our nakedness.
exile us from our laughter
give us this day our rest from seduction
peeling us down to our veins.

and the tower was like no other.   amen.
and the streets escaped under the
cover of darkness   amen.
and the voices called out from
their wounds   amen.
and the fire circumcised the city   amen.

7.

who anointeth this city with napalm?   (I say)

who giveth this city in holy infanticide?

8.

beyond the mornings and afternoons

and deaths detonating the city.

beyond the tourist roadhouses

trading in lobotomies

there is a glimpse of earth

this prodigal earth.

beyond edicts and commandments

commissioned by puritans

there are people

navigating the breath of hurricanes,

beyond concerts and football

and mummers strutting their

sequined processionals.

there is this earth. this country. this city.

this people.

collecting skeletons from waiting rooms

lying in wait. for honor and peace.

one day.

Poem

South African
children braided
in a colony
of charred scarecrows

Morning raga: 6/28/84

did you see the news tonite?
James r. thornwell died today
of an epileptic fit. 41 year old
blackman. ex/ vietnam/veteran.
given lsd in the service spliced
his own genes reproduced himself
in manic depressive colors and
was discharged. jasrthornwell
died today. never worked again.
became a drifter. while his mind
drilled in military sermons and
drugs stepped out of his immaculate
flesh and hummed . . .

Philadelphia: Spring, 1985

1.
/a phila. fireman reflects after
seeing a decapitated body in the MOVE ruins/

to see those eyes
orange like butterflies
over the walls.

i must move away
from this little-ease
where the pulse
shrinks into itself
and carve myself in white.

O to press the seasons
and taste the quiet juice
of their veins.

2. */memory/*
   a.
Thus in the varicose town
where eyes splintered the night with glass
the children touched at random
sat in places where legions rode.

And O we watched the young birds
stretch the sky
until it streamed white ashes

and O we saw mountains lean on seas
to drink the blood of whales
then wander dumb with their wet bowels.

   b.
Everywhere young
faces breathing in crusts.
breakfast of dreams.
The city, lit by a single fire,
followed the air into disorder.
And the sabbath stones singed our eyes
with each morning's coin.

   c.
Praise of a cureless death they heard
without confessor;
Praise of cathedrals
pressing their genesis from priests;
Praise of wild gulls who came and drank
their summer's milk,
then led them toward the parish snow.

How still the spiderless city.
The earth is immemorial in death.

At the Gallery of La Casa de Las Americas, Habana. Dec. 1984

Picture No. 1
Arnold Belkin: Attica

You say Belkin that the bones
keep regenerating themselves
but these zeromen surrounding us
will they always allow us time to
recruit marrow for our bones
packaged in attica mold.
will we always stitch ourselves
together in time Belkin as these
spacemen jailers freeze their
penises in future containers
to be opened in perpetuity.
Stepping back from your picture
Belkin i remember my last visit
to attica the bullet holes loitering
in the walls the sound of bullets
still circling our eyes.

Picture No. 2
Roberto Malta: Chile: Sin Titulo

Comic strip phantoms polluting
the earth with freudian cartoons
dr seuss daddies in crisis,
bleep bleep bleep
calling all saturdaymorning
redwhiteandblueamerican kids
slig spliggety sploo
calling all yall bloods

comeincomein whereeveryouare
hee. hee. haa. And yo mama too.

They're barbecuing ribs this morning
a good sale on 4th of july ribs today
mothers fetuses at half-price
the little black bastards ain't
worth shit nohow.
sitting on top of the world the
stone people sit like pelicans
holier than time.

it's raining clasped hands again.

the acrobatic preachers have
returned wearing their baggy
pants smiles
in the name of general motors
mcdonalds the pope the father
son and holy ghost.
in the name of holidays and genocide:
parades infanticide and imperialism
we bless this wholewideworld
of sports and what's left over
is up for grabs.
to have prayed for a second coming
and found you waiting in the wings
with sylvester trying to catch tweety-bird.
    i thot i saw a putty cat.
    i diiid see a putty cat.
cmon everybody.
    let's dive for cover.

haiku

for morani and mungu

we make our own
way to birth asking which is
the long walk to death.

shigeko: a hiroshima maiden speaks:

i have been amid organized death that hurried
i have been at sea among charitable waves
i have been forgotten by those who once knew me
i have been alone.
i have been under bleached skies that dropped silver
i have been open flesh replaced by commemorative crusts
i have been taped.
i have been specific among generalities
i have been fed residual death in a bottle
i have been in mourning for sterile faces
i have been obliged.

3 × 3
Carl: a Black man Speaks:

i come from white shadows that hide my indigence
i come from walking streets that are detoured
i come from pushing wagons that do not turn
i come from indifference.
i come from uncut cloth that patterns me
i come from vague violets gift-wrapped by slum parked thoughts
i come from hate.
i come from men who assume no responsibilities
i come from their wives who claw in the darkness
i come from white spit foaming with militant bubbles
i come from hell.

3 × 3
the poet: speaks after silence:

i am going among neutral clouds unpunctured

i am going among men unpolished

i am going to museums unadorned

i am going home.

i am going to charge congenital poverty

i am going to hold young heads in my hands
  and turn them slowly

i am going to cry.

i am going amid striped weaves forever winding

i am going unstyled into a cave

i am going in the bluerain that drowns green crystals

i am going to die.

insomnia

i hear the wind of graves moving the sky.
the hills level their priested black
toward the vehement morning.
pain swears above the city.
from galleries of night
unvarnished dreams ring past these giant cuts
and as i kiss the eunuch moon,
the earth is out of my eyes.

"There is no news from Auschwitz"

New York Times article by A. M. Rosenthal, 1958

along that funeral plain
green wipes away old waves
that rolled the eyes
and tangled flowers veil vile kennel dust
bequeathed to dawns.
the years are done.
the earth bent toward canals bears
sterile bowels repenting woven eyes
while bone-filled drifts that scattered blood
yield other births.
death is not there: no special people
trailing alien dens,
or children moving in the rain of ash
unravelling minds.
life is not there: not even myths that rode
young stallions to a circus tent
and carried torches on a convent wire
beyond the tides.
no other signs that men patrol chained
sheets of sea.
i grieve our empty ships.
there is no news from Auschwitz.

question

for mrs. rinaldi

you wonder if i knew
stephen?
   no more than the
other children racing
in the halls.
    you wonder if
we spoke.
  by chance
   today
he asked me for a
pen
  cil seconds
  on pancakes,
    and when i
tried to breath
back ten years
into his mouth
  i tasted
his morning meal.
    you wonder
if i knew stephen?

words

for mr. and mrs. rinaldi

i saw death
  today
and didn't know what
to do with it.
  obscene/
    yellowish/
      death
lounging on a pennsylvania
farm.
  i screamed at death
    today
but my words ran down
against autumn's
  fast pace.
  i know nothing
of here/
  after songs
    of space/filled with souls.
i know only
  that children bloom
    and fade like
      flowers
and that death is a six
o'clock door
  forever changing time.

the inmate

i shall go home today. i am not laughing
my brain is done with dividing the
hilarious from the humorous, i
shall sit at this desk of sanity and
never clean the curtained windows of
a red room where decorated fingers
punctured my intangible reflexes,
i am quiet as the frail green recently
promoted from her cell of frosts. i am
calm as the spreading rain of spring paints
new stripes toward reclaimed targets.
O this white rain will flood the vacant rooms
once leased by reserved apparitions.
i shall go home today and all i require
is tall boots before i disturb the grounded
snow that alerts me.

Last recording session/for papa Joe

don't be so mean papa
cuz the music don't come easily now
don't stomp the young dude
straining over his birthright.
he don't know what he doing yet
his mornings are still comin
one at a time
don't curse the night papa joe
cuz yo beat done run down
we still hear yo fierce tides
yo midnight caravans singing tongues into morning,
don't be so mean man
one day he'll feel the thunder in yo/ hands
yo/arms wide as the sea
outrunning the air defiantly.
you been ahead so long
can't many of us even now
follow the scent you done left behind.
don't be so mean man un less
you mean
   to be mean
      to be
        me
when you mean
     to be
       mean.

tanka

for papa Joe Jones who
used to toss me up to the sky

sailing upward i
crease the air see you look a/
way. yo spastic arms
in conversation with the day
turn to catch my yellow lips.

haiku
(walking in the rain in Guyana)

watusi like trees
holding the day like green um/
brellas catching rain.

on listening to Malcolm's Ballot or The Bullet

make it plain brother
malcolm sweet singer
of tongues that loosen
the scalp. show me how
to be a revolutionary
overnight. wrap me in your
red orange rage
til i ripen in your black field.
O masculine man of words
your words run down
and no one can wind
you up again.

Song No. 3

for 2nd & 3rd grade sisters

cain't nobody tell me any different
i'm ugly and you know it too
you just smiling to make me feel better
but i see how you stare when nobody's watching you.

i know i'm short black and skinny
and my nose stopped growin fo it wuz 'posed to
i know my hairs short, legs and face ashy
and my clothes have holes that run right through to you.

so i sit all day long just by myself
so i jump the sidewalk cracks knowin i cain't fall
cuz who would want to catch someone who looks like me
who ain't even cute or even just a little tall.

cain't nobody tell me any different
i'm ugly anybody with sense can see.
but. one day i hope somebody will stop me and say
looka here. a pretty little black girl lookin' just like me.

Dear Mama,

It is Christmas eve and the year is passing away with calloused feet. My father, your son and I decorate the night with words. Sit ceremoniously in human song. Watch our blue sapphire words eclipse the night. We have come to this simplicity from afar.

He stirs, pulls from his pocket a faded picture of you. Blackwoman. Sitting in frigid peace. All of your biography preserved in your face. And my eyes draw up short as he says, "Her name was Elizabeth but we used to call her Lizzie." And I hold your picture in my hands. But I know your name by heart. It's Mama. I hold you in my hands and let time pass over my face: "Let my baby be. She ain't like the others. She rough. She'll stumble on gentleness later on."

Ah Mama. Gentleness ain't never been no stranger to my genes. But I did like the roughness of running and swallowing the wind, diving in rivers I could barely swim, jumping from second story windows into a saving backyard bush. I did love you for loving me so hard until I slid inside your veins and sailed your blood to an uncrucified shore.

And I remember Saturday afternoons at our house. The old sister deaconesses sitting in sacred pain. Black cadavers burning with lost aromas. And I crawled behind the couch and listened to breaths I had never breathed. Tasted their enormous martyrdom. Lives spent on so many things. Heard their laughter at Sister Smith's latest performance in church—her purse sailing toward Brother Thomas's head again. And I hugged the laughter round my knees. Draped it round my shoulder like a Spanish shawl.

And history began once again. I received it and let it circulate in my blood. I learned on those Saturday afternoons about women rooted in themselves, raising themselves in dark America, discharging their pain without ever stopping. I learned about women fighting men back when they hit them: "Don't never let no mens hit you mo than once girl." I learned about "womens waking up they mens" in the nite with pans of hot grease and the compromises reached after the smell of hot grease had penetrated their sleepy brains. I learned about loose women walking their abandoned walk down front in church, crossing their legs instead of their hands to God. And I crept into my eyes. Alone with my daydreams of being woman. Adult. Powerful. Loving. Like them. Allowing nobody to rule me if I didn't want to be.

And when they left. When those old bodies had gathered up their sovereign smells. After they had kissed and packed up beans snapped and cakes cooked and laughter bagged. After they had called out their last goodbyes, I crawled out of my place. Surveyed the room. Then walked over to the couch where some had sat for hours and bent my head and smelled their evening smells. I screamed out loud, "oooweeee! Ain't that stinky!" and I laughed laughter from a thousand corridors. And you turned Mama, closed the door, chased me round the room until I crawled into a corner where your large body could not reach me. But your laughter pierced the little alcove where I sat laughing at the night. And your humming sprinkled my small space. Your humming about your Jesus and how one day he was gonna take you home . . .

Because you died when I was six Mama, I never laughed like that again. Because you died without warning Mama, my sister and I moved from family to stepmother to friend of the family. I never felt your warmth again.

But I knew corners and alcoves and closets where I was pushed when some mad woman went out of control. Where I sat for days while some woman raved in rhymes about unwanted children. And work. And not enough money. Or love. And I sat out my childhood with stutters and poems gathered in my head like some winter storm. And the poems erased the stutters and pain. And the words loved me and I loved them in return.

My first real poem was about you Mama and death. My first real poem recited an alphabet of spit splattering a white bus driver's face after he tried to push cousin Lucille off a bus and she left Birmingham under the cover of darkness. Forever. My first real poem was about your Charles-white arms holding me up against death.

My life flows from you Mama. My style comes from a long line of Louises who picked me up in the nite to keep me from wetting the bed. A long line of Sarahs who fed me and my sister and fourteen other children from watery soups and beans and a lot of imagination. A long line of Lizzies who made me understand love. Sharing. Holding a child up to the stars. Holding your tribe in a grip of love. A long line of Black people holding each other up against silence.

I still hear your humming Mama. The color of your song calls me home. The color of your words saying, "Let her be. She got a right to be different. She gonna stumble on herself one of these days. Just let the child be."

And I be Mama.

Fall

i have been drunk since
summer, sure you would
come to sift the waves
until they flaked like
diamonds over our flanks.
i have not moved
even when wild
horses, with snouts like pigs,
came to violate me,
i squatted in
my baptism.
O hear the sea
galloping like stallions
toward spring.

short poem: at midnite

however i secure my life
whenever i drink or eat
whatever i sense through the doors of my head
my luck is short like dust.
whenever i meet my eyes in travel
whomever i love
wherever i taste the world
my life blushes red.

short poem 3

was it yesterday we shifted the air
and made it blossom?
O the raucous petals loud as a prairie song.
what was the elaborate sweat,
the picnics of the poor
the eyes that clapped the silence?
where was the wisdom of breaths contained
in straw?
O is it you now
pausing in profile inspecting
my wolf dreams?

haiku

for mungu and morani
and the children of soweto

may yo seasons be
long with endless green streets and
permanent summer legs.

haiku

for john brown

man of stainedglass legs
harvesting the blood of Nat
in a hangman's noose.

A poem for my most Intelligent
10:30 am Class/ Fall, 1985

it was autumn. the day insistent
as rust. the city standing
at the edge of confessionals.
I had come to this room from other
rooms. footsteps walking from
under my feet. and i saw
your faces eavesdropping on shadows
rinsing the assassins from your eyes.
and our legs genuflected
beyond pain. incest. rage. and
we turned corners where the scare
crow smiles of priapus would never
dominate. and we braided our
tongues with sequins gathered
up our mothers' veins in
skirts of incense. what we
know now is that the coming spring
will not satisfy this thirst.

Haiku

for Paul Robeson

Your voice unwrapping
Itself from congo
contagious as shrines.

Africa Poem No. 4

Another year. Children dying
wholesale in the streets
outlawed thoughts: arms
for youth. Guerrilla warfare.
No crucifixion to confuse our young.
Land of adulteries.
Let us send guns to explode indulgencies.
No frontal checks.
Turning in my thirst
i see cities heavy
with abortions.
I tap it and tase
our flow. Sweet. Wasted
tapestry. Ah then an
end to sibilants. Blessed
are the warriors who
multiply. Together. We
will string our seeds
like viruses.

style no. 1

i come from a long line of rough mamas.

so here i was walking down market street. coming out of a city hall meeting. night wind at my back, dressed in my finest. black cashmere coat caressing the rim of my gray suede boots. hat sitting acey duecy. anointing the avenue with my black smell.

and this old dude. red as his car inching its way on the sidewalk. honked his horn. slid his body almost out of his skin. toward me. psst. psst. hey. let's you and me have some fun. psst. psst. mon babe. don't you want some of this?

and he pulled his penis out of his pants. held the temporal wonder of men in his hands.

i stopped. looked at him. a memory from deep in the eye. a memory of saturday afternoon moviehouses where knowledge comes with a tremulous cry. old white men. spiderlike. spinning their webs towards young girls legs and out budabbott and loucostello smiles melted. and we moved in the high noon walk of black girls. smelling the breath of an old undertow.

and i saw mama Dixon. dancing on his head. mama Dixon. big loud friend of the family. who stunned us with her curses and liquor. being herself. whose skin breathed hilarious breaths. and i greased my words on her tongue. and she gave them back to me like newly tasted wine.

motha fucka. you offend the night i said. you look like an old mole coming out of its hole. take yo slimy sad ole ass home. fo you get what's coming to you. and yo generation. ask yo mama to skin you. that is if you have had one cuz anybody ugly as you couldna been born.

and i turned my eyes eastward. toward the garage. waking up the incipient night with my steps. ready for the short days. the wind singing in my veins.

Graduation Notes

for Mungu, Morani, Monica and Andrew and Crefeld seniors

So much of growing up is an unbearable waiting. A constant longing for another time. Another season.

I remember walking like you today down this path. In love with the day. Flesh awkward. I sang at the edge of adolescence and the scent of adulthood rushed me and I thought I would suffocate. But I didn't. I am here. So are you. Finally. Tired of tiny noises your eyes hum a large vibration.

I think all journeys are the same. My breath delighting in the single dawn. Yours. Walking at the edge. Unafraid. Anxious for the unseen dawns are mixing today like the underground rhythms seeping from your pores.

At this moment your skins living your eighteen years suspend all noises. Your days still half-opened, crackle like the fires to come. Outside. The earth. Wind. Night. Unfold for you. Listen to their sounds. They have sung me seasons that never abandoned me. A dance of summer rain. A ceremony of thunder waking up the earth to human monuments.

Facing each other I smile at your faces. Know you as young heroes soon to be decorated with years. Hope no wars dwarf you. Know your dreams wild and sweet will sail from your waists to surround the non-lovers. Dreamers. And you will rise up like newborn armies refashioning lives. Louder than the sea you come from.

from Generations

From a Black Feminist Conference Reflections on Margaret Walker: Poet

chicago/october 1977/saturday afternoon/
margaret walker walks her red clay mississippi walk
into a room of feminists. a strong gust of a woman,
raining warm honeysuckle kisses and smiles. and i
fold myself into her and hear a primordial black
song sailing down the guinea coast.

her face. ordained with lines. confesses poems.
halleluyas. choruses. she turns leans her crane like
neck on the edge of the world, emphasizing us.
in this hotel/village/room. heavy with women. our
names become known to us.

there is an echo about her. of black people rhyming
of a woman celebrating herself and a people. words
ripen on her mouth like pomegranates. this pecan/
color/woman. short limbed with lightning. and i
swallow her whole as she pulls herself up from
youth, shaking off those early chicago years where
she and wright and others turned a chicago desert
into a well spring of words.

eyes. brilliant/solution eyes torpedoing the room
with sun. eyes/dressed like a woman. seeing thru
riddles. offering asylum from ghosts.

she stands over centuries as she talks. hands on
waist. a feminine memory washed up from another
shore. she opens her coat. a light colored blouse

dances against dark breasts. her words carved from
ancestral widows rain children and the room
contracts with color.

her voice turns the afternoon brown. this black
woman poet. removing false veils, baptizes us with
syllables. woman words. entering and leaving at
will:

> Let a new earth rise. Let another world be born.
> Let a bloody peace be written in the sky. Let a
> second generation full of courage issue forth; let
> a people loving freedom come to growth. Let a
> beauty full of healing and a strength of final
> clenching be the pulsing in our spirits and our
> blood. Let the martial songs be written, let the
> dirges disappear. Let a race of men now rise and
> take control. *

walking back to my room, i listen to the afternoon.
play it again and again. scatter myself over evening
walls and passageways wet with her footprints.
in my room i collect papers. breasts. and listen
to our mothers hummmmming

---

*"For My People" by Margaret Walker

Reflections After the June 12th March for Disarmament

I have come to you tonite out of the depths
  of slavery
  from white hands peeling black skins over.
  america;
I have come out to you from reconstruction eyes
  that closed on black humanity
  that reduced black hope to the dark
  huts of america;
I have come to you from the lynching years,
  the exploitation of black men and women by
  a country that allowed the swinging of
  strange fruits from southern trees;
I have come to you tonite thru the
  delaney years, the du bois years, the
  b.t. washington years, the robeson
  years, the garvey years, the
  depression years, the you can't eat
  or sit or live just die here years,
  the civil rights years, the black power
  years, the black nationalist years, the
  affirmative action years, the liberal
  years, the neo-conservative years;
I have come to say that those years
  were not in vain, the ghosts of our
  ancestors searching this american dust for
  rest were not in vain, black women
  walking their lives in clots were not
  in vain;

I have come to you tonite as an equal,
  as a comrade, as a black woman
  walking down a corridor of tears,
  looking neither to the left nor the right,
  pulling my history with bruised
  heels,
  beckoning to the illusion of america
  daring you to look me in the eyes to
  see these faces, the exploitation of a
  people because of skin pigmentation;
I have come to you tonite because no people
  have been asked to be modern day people
  with the history of slavery, and still
  we walk, and still we talk, and
  still we plan, and still we hope and
  still we sing;
I have come to you tonite because there are
  inhumanitarians in the world. they are not
  new. they are old. they go back into history.
  they were called explorers, soldiers, mercenaries,
  imperialists, missionaries, adventurers,
  but they looked at the world for what
  it would give up to them and they violated
  the land and the people, they looked
  at the land and sectioned it up for
  private ownership, they looked at the
  people and decided how to manipulate
  them thru fear and ignorance, they looked
  at the gold and began to hoard and
  worship it;

I have come to you because it is time
for us all to purge capitalism from
our dreams, to purge materialism
from our eyes, from the planet earth
to deliver the earth again into the hands
of the humanitarians:
I have come to you tonite not just for the stoppage
of nuclear proliferation, nuclear
plants, nuclear bombs, nuclear
waste, but to stop the proliferation
of nuclear minds, of nuclear generals
of nuclear presidents, of nuclear scientists,
who spread human and nuclear waste
over the world;
I come to you because the world needs to be
saved for the future generations who must
return the earth to peace, who will not
be startled by a man's/woman's skin color;
I come to you because the world needs sanity
now, needs men and women who will
now work to produce nuclear weapons,
who will give up their need for excess
wealth and learn how to share the
world's resources, who will never
again as scientists invent again just
for the sake of inventing;
I come to you because we need to turn our
eyes to the beauty of this planet, to the
bright green laughter of trees, to the beautiful
human animals waiting to smile their
unprostituted smiles;

I have come to you to talk about our inexperience
   at living as human beings, thru death marches
   and camps,
   thru middle passages and slavery
   and thundering countries raining hungry faces;
I am here to move against
   leaving our shadows implanted on the
   earth while our bodies disintegrate in
   nuclear lightning;
I am here between the voices of our ancestors
   and the noise of the planet,
   between the surprise of death and life;
l am here because I shall not give the
   earth up to non-dreamers and earth molesters;
I am here to say to you:
   my body is full of veins
   like the bombs waiting to burst
   with blood.
   we must learn to suckle life not
   bombs and rhetoric
   rising up in redwhiteandblue patriotism;
I am here. and my breath/our breaths
   must thunder across this land
   arousing new breaths. new life.
   new people, who will live in peace
   and honor.

A Poem of Praise

*for Gerald Penny who died September 21, 1973, Amherst College/
und for the Brothers of Amherst College*

Man
is an alien in this world
in spite of all the pleasures.

Man is an early traveler
who tastes in himself
the world.

When you wake up in the morning — Man.
meditate on your beginning
meditate as you flow in
the waters of your birth
meditate on the nine months
you rest unseen
and the world awaits you
when you come soiled and crying.
And they pick you up
like one small melon
and hush up
your crying.

At first you do not speak
and your legs are like orphans
at first your two eyes cross
themselves in confusion
at first your mouth knows only
the full breasts of milk
a sweet taste of this world.

There is nothing which does not come to an end
And to live one year is good in the sight of God.

You are born
worthy of praise
all things that HE
makes are worthy of praise.

In your days made up of dreams
in your eyes made of dawn
you walked toward old age,
child of the rainbow
child of beauty
through the broad fields
and your eyes gained power
and your limbs grew long like yellow corn
an abundance of life
an abundance of joy
with beauty before you, you walked
toward old age.

There is nothing which does not come to an end
And to live seven years is good in the sight of God.

Silently to life
you spoke
young male child.

You praised life
coming as a river between hills
and your laughter
was like red berries in summer
and your shouting like giant eagles

As you walked toward old age
young male child
your voice harnessed the wind

There is nothing which does not come to an end
And to live fourteen years is good in the sight of God.

Father.
behold me
in a sacred manner.

Mother,
behold me
in a sacred manner.

My family sitting holy.
behold me
in a sacred manner.

For i am man
and i must
run with the evening tide
must hold up my hands
for my life is opening
before me.

I am going to walk far to the East
i hope to find a good morning
somewhere.

I am going to race my own voice
i hope to have peace
somewhere.

Father, Mother.
behold me now.
i have moved to a
House of Darkness
but your memories of me
light my way.

I do not cry
for i am man
no longer
a child of your
womb.

There is nothing which does not
        come to an end
And to live seventeen years is good
        in the sight of God.

Father and Daughter

we talk of light things you and I in this
small house. no winds stir here among
flame orange drapes that drape our genesis
And snow melts into rivers. The young
grandchild reviews her impudence that
makes you laugh and clap for more allure.
Ah, how she twirls the emerald lariat.
When evening comes your eyes transfer
to space you have not known and taste the blood
breath of a final flower. Past equal birth,
the smell of salt begins another flood:
your land is in the ashes of the South.
perhaps the color of our losses:
perhaps the memory that dreams nurse:
old man, we do not speak of crosses.

9

from

Homegirls and Handgrenades

Story

in medias res
there came a man into the city
he wore a jackdaw face
and loved the glittering town.
i cannot say why he chose me.
i was the city's device
the city's kept disgrace.
yet he lifted me until i had
a passion to please
all displeasures.

each day he said
o my child,
the world has moved away from love
the earth has moved away from worship
i am destined to end their exile.

         and he returned me to the mainland
         dressed in white. i was in unity.
         soon, o soon, i would be worthy.

because he was good with his hands
he became a technician
where mathematical abstractions
were operable.
thus he caressed two levers that could level
three generations of russians
resting in their squares.

each day he cried
when will they understand the
errors of their ways

when will they touch the godhead
and leave the verses of the rocks?
                    and i was dressed in blue
                    blue of the savior's sky
                    soon, o soon i would be worthy.
there are many cities
there are men in the cities
rooted.
there are few men
there are few cities
afraid.
there are cities
crowded with christs
invisible
there are men
crystal with echoes
indifferent
there are many cities
there are men in the cities
empty
there are few cities
there are few men
worthy.

                    soon, o soon, I would be worthy.

ringaroundtheatmosphere
apocketfullofchains
kerboomkerboom
wehavenopains

Poem Written After Reading Wright's "American Hunger"

for the homegirl who told Wright of her desire to go to the circus

such a simple desire
wanting to go to the circus
wanting to see the animals
orange with laughter.

such a simple need
amid yo /easy desire
to ride her
while clowns waited offstage
and children tugged at her young legs.

did you tell her man that we're
all acrobats tumbling out of
our separate arenas?
you. peeling her
skin while dreams turned
somersaults in her eyes.

such a simple woman
illiterate with juices
in a city where hunger
is passed around for seconds.

A Song

take my virginity
and convert it to maternity
wait around a century or two
and see just what I'll do.

take my body give it yo' brand
stitch my breasts on the fatherland
wait around a decade or two
and see just what i'll do.

place my dreams on any back stair
tune my eyes for yo' nightmare
wait around a century or two
and see what I'll finally do.

suck my breath until i stutter
listen to the sounds i utter
wait around a decade or two
and see just what i'll do.

take my daughter one sunday morn
drape her in dresses to be torn
wait around a century or two
and see what i'll finally do.

all dressed in white
find yourself a brand new wife
wait around a decade or two
and see what she'll finally do.
and see what she'll finally do.

Haiku

i see you blackboy
bent toward destruction watching
for death with tight eyes

Masks

"blacks don't have the intellectual capacity to succeed."
WILLIAM COORS

the river runs toward day
and never stops.
so life receives the lakes
patrolled by one-eyed pimps
who wash their feet in our blue whoredom

the river floods
the days grow short
we wait to change our masks
we wait for warmer days and
fountains without force
we wait for seasons without power.

today
ah today
only the shrill sparrow seeks the sky
our days are edifice.
we look toward temples that give birth to sanctioned flesh.

           o bring the white mask
              full of the chalk sky.

entering the temple
on this day of sundays
i hear the word spoken
by the unhurried speaker
who speaks of unveiled eyes.

           o bring the chalk mask
              full of altitudes.

straight in this chair
tall in an unrehearsed role
i rejoice
and the spirit sinks in twilight of
distant smells.

                                          o bring the mask
                                          full of drying blood.

fee, fie, fo, fum,
i smell the blood
of an englishman

O my people
wear the white masks
for they speak without speaking
and hear words of forgetfulness.

o my people.

A Poem for Paul

your face like
summer lightning
gets caught in my voice
and i draw you up from
deep rivers
taste your face of a
thousand names
see you smile
a new season
hear your voice
a wild sea pausing in the wind.

Bubba

How shall I tell you of him. Bubba, young man of Harlem? Bubba. Of filling stations and handball games; of summer bongo playing; of gang bangs; of strict laughter piercing the dark, long summers kept us peeled across stoops looking for air. Bubba. Of gangs who pimped a long walk across Harlem and decided who would pass and who would be stopped at the gateway of life.

Bubba. Black as a panther. Bubba. Whose teeth shone like diamonds while he smiled at us from across his dominion. Who stretched his legs until they snapped in two when his days became shorter and schools sent him out among the world of pushcarts and do rags of Seventh Avenue. Bubba. Who gave his genius up to the temper of the times.

While I marched off to Hunter College and the aroma of Park Avenue; while I marched off to Proust and things unremembered; while I read sociology texts that reminded us few Blacks that we were aberrations of the world; Bubba, and other marched off to days of living in a country that said, "I'm the greatest hustler in the world so don't come downtown trying to hustle me. Hustle your own."

And he did. And they did.

"Hey there, pretty lady. Yeah. You strutting yo' young black ass 'cross 125th street. I be digging on you. See that corner over there baby? Stretch out on that corner so we can live in the style that we ain't never been accustomed to. Want to be accustomed to."

And she did. And they did. Young girls throwing their souls on Harlem corners. Standing dead on dead avenues. Caged black birds in a country without age or memory.

One summer day, I remember Bubba and I banging the ball against the filling station. Handball champs we were. The king and queen of the handball we were. And we talked as we played. He asked me if I ever talked to trees or rivers or things like that, and I who walked with voices for years denied the different tongues populating my mouth. I stood still denying the commonplace things of my private childhood. And his eyes pinned me against the filling station wall and my eyes became small and lost their color.

"I hear voices all the time," he said. "I talk to the few trees we have here in Harlem." And then he smiled a smile that kept moving back to some distant time that I stopped looking at him and turned away. I thought I would get lost inside his sorcery.

"When I was real small," he continued, "I used to think that the moon belonged to me, that it came out only for me, that it followed me everywhere I went. And I used to, when it got dark there in North Carolina, I used to run around to the backyard and wait for the moon to appear. And when she came out I would dance a wild dance that woke up my father. My father used to scream outside at me and say, 'Stop that foolishness boy. You ain't got the sense you wuz born with.'" Bubba laughed a laugh that came from a million cells.

"I ain't never told nobody that before. But you so dreamylike girl, always reading, that I thought you would know what it is to walk with drums beating inside you. But you just a brain with no imagination at all. Catch ya later baby. I'm gon go on downtown to a flick."

I nodded my head as he left. I nodded my head as I hit the ball against the wall. I nodded my head as the voices peeped in and out of my ears and nostrils leaving a trail around my waist. I picked myself up from the fear of anyone knowing who I was and went home; never to talk to Bubba again about seeing behind trees and walking over seas with flowers growing out of my head.

Words. Books. Waltzed me to the tune of Hunter College days. I severed all relationships with my block. Each night I drenched myself with words so I could burst through the curtain of Harlem days and nights. My banner was my tongue as I climbed toward the gourds of knowledge and recited a poem of life.

"Hey. There. Girl. How you be? Hear you goin' to Hunter now. How is it?" It was Bubba. Bubba. Of greasy overalls. Of two children screaming for food. Of a wife pregnant with another. Of the same old neighborhood.

"Oh, Hunter's all right Bubba. If you like that sort of thing."

"But what you studying girl? What you studying to be? A teacher? A lawyer? What?"

"Well, I'm studying a little Sociology. Psychology. History. Chemistry. I'm not quite sure just what it is I intend to be. Do you understand?"

"Yeah, I understand. Catch you later girl." And he walked his tired footsteps to the corner bar and went inside.

And I stood outside. Afraid to cross the street, abandoned to the rhythms of America's tom-toms.

One day, after graduation, I returned to the old neighborhood. I recognized a few faces and sat and talked. I was glad to sit down. I had taught all day long. I answered the questions of my former neighbors. And the tension of the years dissolved in our laughter. Just people. Remembering together. Laughing.

"Does Bubba still live 'round here?" I finally asked. The women pointed to the mini-park. And I called out goodbye and walked past the filling station to the park. There he sat. Nodding out the day. The years.

As long as I have hands that write; as long as I have eyes that see; as long as I can bear your name against silence; I shall never forget our last talk Bubba. That September day when I sat next to you and told you my dreams and my prayers.

The air froze as you raised your hand and spoke. "Hey there girl. How . . ." And I continued to talk. Holding your hand, our silence, remembering for you the laughter you gave us so freely, thanking you for the conversations and protection you gave me.

"Hey there girl," he sniffled. "Wanna play some handball and . . ."

And I waited with him on that bench. Watched the sun go down. Saw the moon come out.

"Bubba," I said. "There she is, your old friend the moon. Coming out just for you."

He finally pulled himself up off the bench. He stood up with the last breath of a dying man.

"How 'bout a few bucks girl? Gotta see a man 'bout something."

I handed him $20. He put it in his pocket, scratched his legs and nodded goodbye.

Bubba. If you hadn't fallen off of that roof in '57, you would have loved the '60s. Bubba you would have loved Malcolm. You would have plucked the light from his eyes and finally seen the world in focus.

Bubba. Your footsteps sing around my waist each day. I will not let the country settle into the sleep of the innocent.

A Letter to Dr. Martin Luther King

Dear Martin,

Great God, what a morning, Martin!

The sun is rolling in from faraway places. I watch it reaching out, circling these bare trees like some reverent lover, I have been standing still listening to the morning, and I hear your voice crouched near hills, rising from the mountain tops, breaking the circle of dawn.

You would have been 54 today.

As I point my face toward a new decade, Martin, I want you to know that the country still crowds the spirit. I want you to know that we still hear your footsteps setting out on a road cemented with black bones. I want you to know that the stuttering of guns could not stop your light from crashing against cathedrals chanting piety while hustling the world.

Great God, what a country, Martin!

The decade after your death docked like a spaceship on a new planet. Voyagers all we were. We were the aliens walking up the '70s, a holocaust people on the move looking out from dark eyes. A thirsty generation, circling the peaks of our country for more than a Pepsi taste. We were youngbloods, spinning hip syllables while saluting death in a country neutral with pain.

And our children saw the mirage of plenty spilling from capitalistic sands.

And they ran toward the desert.

And the gods of sand made them immune to words that strengthen the breast.

And they became scavengers walking on the earth.

And you can see them playing. Hide-and-go-seek robbers. Native sons. Running on their knees. Reinventing slavery on asphalt. Peeling their umbilical cords for a gold chain.

And you can see them on Times Square, in N.Y.C., Martin, selling their 11-, 12-year-old, 13-, 14-year-old bodies to suburban forefathers.

And you can see them on Market Street in Philadelphia bobbing up bellywise, young fishes for old sharks,

And no cocks are crowing on those mean streets.

Great God, what a morning it'll be someday, Martin!

That decade fell like a stone on our eyes. Our movements. Rhythms. Loves. Books. Delivered us from the night, drove out the fears keeping some of us hoarse. New births knocking at the womb kept us walking.

We crossed the cities while a backlash of judges tried to turn us into moles with blackrobed words of reverse racism. But we knew. And our knowing was like a sister's embrace. We crossed the land where famine was fed in public. Where black stomachs exploded on the world's dais while men embalmed their eyes and tongues in gold. But we knew. And our knowing squatted from memory.

Sitting on our past, we watch the new decade dawning. These are strange days, Martin, when the color of freedom becomes disco fever; when soap operas populate our Zulu braids; as the world turns to the conservative right and general hospitals are closing in Black neighborhoods and the young and the restless are drugged by early morning reefer butts. And houses tremble.

These are dangerous days, Martin, when cowboy-riding presidents corral Blacks (and others) in a common crown of thorns; when nuclear-toting generals recite an alphabet of blood; when multinational corporations assassinate ancient cultures while inaugurating new civilizations. Come out come out, wherever you are. Black country. Waiting to be born . . .

But, Martin, on this, your 54th birthday—with all the reversals—we have learned that black is the beginning of everything.

it was black in the universe before the sun;

it was black in the mind before we opened our eyes;

it was black in the womb of our mother;

black is the beginning,

and if we are the beginning we will be forever.

Martin. I have learned too that fear is not a Black man or woman.

Fear cannot disturb the length of those who struggle against material gains for self-aggrandizement. Fear cannot disturb the good of people who have moved to a meeting place where the pulse pounds out freedom and justice for the universe.

Now is the changing of the tides, Martin. You forecast it where leaves dance on the wings of man. Martin. Listen. On this your 54th year, listen and you will hear the earth delivering up curfews to the missionaries and assassins. Listen. And you will hear the tribal songs:

Ayeeee	*Ayooooo*	*Ayeee*
Ayeeee	*Ayooooo*	*Ayeee*

Malcolm . . .	*Ke wa rona**
Robeson . . .	*Ke wa rona*
Lumumba . . .	*Ke wa rona*
Fannie Lou . . .	*Ke wa rona*
Garvey . . .	*Ke wa rona*
Johnbrown . . .	*Ke wa rona*
Tubman . . .	*Ke wa rona*
Mandela . . .	*Ke wa rona*

(free Mandela,

free Mandela)

Ássata . . .	*Ke wa rona*

As we go with you to the sun,

as we walk in the dawn, turn our eyes

Eastward and let the prophecy come true

and let the prophecy come true.

Great God, Martin, what a morning it will be!

---

*Ke wa rona: he is ours

MIAS

(missing in action and other atlantas)

this morning i heard the cuckoo bird calling
and i saw children wandering like quicksand
over the exquisite city
scooping up summer leaves in enema bags
self-sustaining warriors spitting
long metal seeds on porcelain bricks.

atlanta:

     city of cathedrals and colleges
     rustling spirituals in the morning air
     while black skulls splinter the nite
     and emmett till bones drop in choruses.

littleman. where you running to?
yes. you. youngblood.
touching and touched at random
running towards places where legions ride.

     yo man. you want some action.
     im yo/main man.
     buy me. i can give it to you
     wholesale.

heyladycarryyobagsfoyou?
50¢costyouonly50¢.yo.man.
washyocar.idoagoodjob.
heymanwhyyousocold?
yoman.youneedyobasement
cleaned?meandmypartner
doyoupdecent. yoman.

johannesburg:

       squatting like a manicured mannequin
       while gathering ghosts clockwise
       and policing men, using up their tongues
       Pronounce death syllables
       in the nite,

       august 18:
       30 yr. old african arrested
       on the highway. taken to
       port elizabeth. examined.
       found to be in good health.
       placed in a private cell
       for questioning.

       sept. 7:
       varicose cells. full of
       assassins, beating their
       red arms against the walls.
       and biko, trying to ration
       his blood spills permanent
       blood in a port elizabeth cell.
       and biko's body sings heavy
       with cracks.

       sept. 13:
       hear ye. hear ye. hear ye.
       i regret to announce that stephen
       biko is dead. he has refused
       food since sept. 5th. we did
       all we could for the man.

he has hanged himself while sleeping
we did all we could for him.
he fell while answering our questions
we did all we could for the man.
he washed his face and hung him
self out to dry
we did all we could for him.
he drowned while drinking his supper
we did all we could for the man.
he fell

        hangedhimself   starved
drowned himself
we did all we could for him.
it's hard to keep someone alive
who won't even cooperate.
hear ye.

can i borrow yo/eyes south africa?
can i redistribute yo/legs america?
multiplying multinationally over the world.

    yebo madoda*
    yebo bafazi
    i say
    yebo madoda
    yebo bafazi

el salvador:
    country of vowelled ghosts.
    country of red bones
    a pulse beat gone mad
    with death.

---

yebo madoda: come on men and women

redwhiteandblue guns splintering the nite with glass
redwhiteandblue death squads running on borrowed
knees cascading dreams.

quiero ser libre
pues libre naci
    i say
quiero ser libre
pues libre naci

they came to the village that nite. all day the
birds had pedaled clockwise drowning their
feet in clouds. the old men and women
talked of foreboding, that it was a bad sign.
and they crossed themselves in two as
their eyes concluded design.
they came that nite to the village.
calling peace. liberty. freedom.
their tongues lassoing us with
circus patriotism
their elbows wrapped in blood paper
they came penises drawn
their white togas covering their
stained glass legs
their thick hands tattooing decay
on los campaneros till their
young legs rolled out from under them
to greet death
they came leaving a tattoo of hunger
over the land.
    quiero ser libre
    pues libre naci
so i plant myself in the middle
of my biography

of dying drinking working dancing people
their tongues swollen with slavery
waiting and i say
yebo madoda
yebo bafazi
cmon men and women
peel your guerrilla veins toward
this chorus line of beasts who will sell
the morning air passing thru your bones
cmon. men. and. women.
plant yourself in the middle of your
blood with no transfusions for
reagan or botha or bush or
d'aubuisson.

plant yourself in the eyes of
the children who have died carving out their
own childhood.
plant yourself in the dreams of the people
scattered by morning bullets.
let there be everywhere our talk.
let there be everywhere our eyes.
let there be everywhere our thoughts.
let there be everywhere our love.
let there be everywhere our actions.
breathing hope and victory
into their unspoken questions
summoning the dead to life again
to the hereafter of freedom.

cmon. men. women,
i want to be free.

On Seeing a Pacifist Burn

this day is not
real. the crowing of
the far-away
carillons ring
out direction
less. even you are
un real roasting
under a man
hattan sky
while passersby flap
their indecent tongues.
even i am un
real but i
am black and
thought to be
without meaning.

Letter to Ezekiel Mphahlele

dear zeke,

i've just left your house where you and rebecca served a dinner of peace to me and my sons. the ride home is not as long as the way i came, two centuries of hunger brought me along many detours before i recognized your house. it is raining and as i watch the raindrops spin like colored beads on the windshield, i hear your voice calling out to your ancestors to prepare a place for you, for you were returning home leaving the skeleton rites of twenty years behind.

you and rebecca have been walking a long time. your feet have crossed the african continent to this western one where you moved amid leaden eyes and laughter that froze you in snow/capped memories. your journey began in 1957, when the ruling class could not understand your yawns of freedom, the motion of a million eyes to see for themselves what life was/is and could be, and you cut across the burial grounds of south africa where many of your comrades slept and you cut across those black africans smiling their long smiles from diplomatic teeth. now you are returning home. now your mother's womb cries out to you. now your history demands your heartbeat. and you turn your body toward the whirlwind of change, toward young black voices calling for a dignity speeding beyond control, on the right side of the road. but this nite full of whispering summer trees, this nite nodding with south african faces, heard you say, sonia. i must be buried in my country in my own homeland, my bones must replenish the black earth from whence they came, our bones must fertilize the ground on which we walk or we shall never walk as men and women in the 21st century.

i talked to my sons as the car chased the longlegged rain running before us. i told them that men and women are measured by their acts not by their swaggering speech or walk, or the money they have stashed between their legs. i talked to my sons about bravery outside of bruce lee grunts and jabs, outside of star wars' knights fertilizing america's green

youth into continued fantasies while reality explodes in neutron bold-
ness. i said you have just sat and eaten amid bravery. relish the taste.
stir it around and around in your mouth until the quick sweetness of it
becomes bitter, then swallow it slowly, letting this new astringent taste
burn the throat. bravery is no easy taste to swallow. i said this man and
woman we have just left this nite have decided to walk like panthers in
their country, to breathe again their own breath suspended by twenty
years of exile, to settle in the maternal space of their birth where there
are men who "shake hands without hearts" waiting for them. they are a
fixed portrait of courage.

it is 2 a.m., my children stretch themselves in dreams, kicking away
the room's shadows. i stare at the nite piling in little heaps near my bed.
zeke. maybe you are a madman. i a madwoman to want to walk across
the sea, to saddle time while singing a future note. we follow the new
day's breath, we answer old bruises waiting to descend upon our heads,
we answer screams creeping out of holes and shells buried by memories
waiting to be cleansed. you invoking the ghosts lurking inside this child/
woman. you breaking my curtain of silence. i love the tom-tom days you
are marching, your feet rooted in the sea. save a space for me and mine
zeke and rebecca. this lost woman, who walks her own shadow for peace.

from

Wounded in the House of a Friend

Part I

*I have only one solution: to rise
above this absurd drama that
others have staged around me.*

FRANTZ FANON

Wounded in the House of a Friend

Set No. 1

> *the unspoken word*
> *is born, i see it in our*
> *eyes dancing*

She hadn't found anything. i had been careful. No lipstick. No matches from a well-known bar. No letters. Cards. Confessing an undying love. Nothing tangible for her to hold onto. But i knew she knew. It had been on her face, in her eyes for the last nine days. It was the way she looked at me sideways from across the restaurant table as she picked at her brown rice sushi. It was the way she paused in profile while inspecting my wolfdreams. It was the way her mouth took a detour from talk. And then as we exited the restaurant she said it quite casually: i know there's another woman. You must tell me about her when we get home.

Yeah. There was another woman. In fact there were three women. In Florida, California, and North Carolina. Places to replace her cool detachment of these last years. No sex for months. Always tired or sick or off to some conference designed to save the world from racism or extinction. If i had jerked off one more time in bed while lying next to her it woulda dropped off. Still i wondered how she knew.

> *am i dressed right for the smoke?*
> *will it wrinkle if i fall?*

i had first felt something was wrong at the dinner party. His colleague's house. He was so animated. The first flush of his new job i thought. He spoke staccato style. Two drinks in each hand. His laughter. Wild. Hard.

238

Contagious as shrines enveloped the room. He was so wired that i thought he was going to explode. i didn't know the people there. They were all lawyers. Even the wives were lawyers. Glib and self-assured. Discussing cases, and colleagues. Then it happened. A small hesitation on his part. In answer to a question as to how he would be able to get some important document from one place to another, he looked at the host and said: They'll get it to me. Don't worry. And the look passing back and forth between the men told of collusion and omission. Told of dependence on other women for information and confirmation. Told of nites i had stretched out next to him and he was soft. Too soft for my open legs. And i turned my back to him and the nites multiplied out loud. As i drove home from the party i asked him what was wrong? What was bothering him? Were we okay? Would we make love tonite? Would we ever make love again? Did my breath stink? Was i too short? Too tall? Did i talk too much? Should i wear lipstick? Should i cut my hair? Let it grow? What did he want for dinner tomorrow nite? Was i driving too fast? Too slow? What is wrong man? He said i was always exaggerating. Imagining things. Always looking for trouble.

Do they have children?
one does.

Are they married?
one is.

They're like you then.
yes.

How old are they?
thirty-two, thirty-three, thirty-four.

What do they do?
an accountant and two lawyers.

They're like you then.
yes.

239

Do they make better love than i do?
i'm not answering that.

Where did you meet?
when i traveled on the job.

Did you make love in hotels?
yes.

Did you go out together?
yes.

To bars? To movies? To restaurants?
yes.

Did you make love to them all nite?
yes.

And then got up to do your company work?
yes.

And you fall asleep on me right after
dinner. After work. After walking the dog.
yes.

Did you buy them things?
yes.

Did you talk on the phone with them every day?
yes.

Do you tell them how unhappy you are
with me and the children?
yes.

Do you love them? Did you say that you
loved them while making love?
i'm not answering that.

can i pull my bones
together while skeletons
come out of my head?

i am preparing for him to come home. i have exercised. Soaked in the tub. Scrubbed my body. Oiled myself down. What a beautiful day it's been. Warmer than usual. The cherry blossoms on the drive are blooming prematurely. The hibiscus are giving off a scent around the house. i have gotten drunk off the smell. So delicate. So sweet. So loving. i have been sleeping, no, daydreaming all day. Lounging inside my head. i am walking up this hill. The day is green. All green. Even the sky. i start to run down the hill and i take wing and begin to fly and the currents turn me upside down and i become young again childlike again ready to participate in all children's games.

She's fucking my brains out. I'm so tired i just want to put my head down at my desk. Just for a minute. What is wrong with her? For one whole month she's turned to me every nite. Climbed on top of me. Put my dick inside her and become beautiful. Almost birdlike. She seemed to be flying as she rode me. Arms extended. Moving from side to side. But my God. Every night. She's fucking my brains out. I can hardly see the morning and I'm beginning to hate the nite.

He's coming up the stairs. i've opened the venetian blinds. i love to see the trees outlined against the night air. Such beauty and space. i have oiled myself down for the night. i slept during the day. He's coming up the stairs. i have been waiting for him all day. i am singing a song i learned years ago. It is pretty like this nite. Like his eyes.

i can hardly keep my eyes open. Time to climb out of bed. Make the 7:20 train. My legs and bones hurt. i'm outta condition. Goddamn it. She's turning my way again. She's smiling. Goddamn it.

What a beautiful morning it is. i've been listening to the birds for the last couple hours. How beautifully they sing. Like sacred music. i got up *and exercised while he slept. Made a cup of green tea. Oiled my body down. Climbed back into bed and began to kiss him all over . . .*

Ted. Man. i'm so tired i can hardly eat this food. But i'd better eat cuz i'm losing weight. You know what man. i can't even get a hard-on when another bitch comes near me. Look at that one there with that see-through skirt on. Nothing. My dick is so limp only she can bring it up. And she does. Every nite. It ain't normal is it for a wife to fuck like she does. Is it man? It ain't normal. Like it ain't normal for a woman you've lived with for twenty years to act like this.

She was killing him. He knew it. As he approached their porch he wondered what it would be tonite. The special dinner. The erotic movie. The whirlpool. The warm oil massage until his body awakened in spite of himself. In spite of an 18 hour day at the office. As he approached the house he hesitated. He had to stay in control tonite. This was getting out of hand.

She waited for him. In the bathroom. She'd be waiting for him when he entered the shower. She'd come in to wash his back. Damn these big walk-in showers. No privacy. No time to wash yourself and dream. She'd come with those hands of hers. Soaking him. On the nipples. Chest. Then she'd travel on down to his thing. He sweet peter jesus. So tired. So forlorn. And she'd begin to tease him. Play with him. Suck him until he rose up like some fucking private first class. Anxious to do battle. And she'd watch him rise until he became Captain Sweet Peter. And she'd climb on him. Close her eyes.

honey. it's too much you know.
What?

all this sex. it's getting so i can't concentrate.
Where?

at the office. at lunch. on the train. on planes.
all i want to do is sleep.
Why?

you know why. every place i go you're there.
standing there. smiling. waiting, touching.
Yes.

in bed. i can't turn over and you're there.
lips open. smiling, all revved up.
Aren't you horny too?

yes. but enough's enough. you're my wife. it's
not normal to fuck as much as you do.
No?

it's not well, nice, to have you talk the way
you talk when we're making love.
No?

can't we go back a little, go back to our
normal life when you just wanted to sleep at
nite and make love every now and then? like me.
No.

what's wrong with you. are you having a nervous
breakdown or something?
No.

> *if i become the*
> *other woman will i be*
> *loved like you loved her?*

And he says i don't laugh. All this he says while he's away in California for one week. But i've been laughing all day. All week. All year. i know what to do now. i'll go outside and give it away. Since he doesn't really want me. My love. My body. When we make love his lips swell up. His legs and arms hurt. He coughs. Drinks water. Develops a strain at his butt-hole. Yeah. What to do now. Go outside and give it away. Pussy. Sweet. Black pussy.

For sale. Wholesale pussy. Right here. Sweet black pussy. Hello there Mr.
Mailman. What's your name again? Oh yes. Harold. Can i call you Harry?
How are you this morning? Would you like some cold water it's so hot out
there. You want a doughnut a cookie some cereal some sweet black pussy?
Oh God. Man. Don't back away. Don't run down the steps. Oh my God he
fell. The mail is all over the sidewalk. hee hee hee. Guess i'd better be more
subtle with the next one. hee hee hee. He's still running down the block.
Mr. Federal Express Man. Cmon over here. Let me Fed Ex you and anyone
else some Sweet Funky Pure Smelling Black Pussy. hee hee hee.

I shall become his collector of small things; become his collector of
burps, biceps and smiles; I shall bottle his farts, frowns and creases; I shall
gather up his moans, words, outbursts wrap them in blue tissue paper; get
to know them; watch them grow in importance; file them in their place
in their scheme of things; I shall collect his scraps of food; ferret them
among my taste buds; allow each particle to saunter into my cells; all
aboard; calling all food particles; cmon board this fucking food express;
climb into these sockets golden with brine; I need to taste him again.

you can't keep his dick in your purse

Preparation for the trip to Dallas. Los Angeles. New Orleans. Bal-
timore. Washington. Hartford. Brownsville. (Orlando. Miami. Late
check-in. Rush. Limited liability.) That's why you missed me at the air-
port. Hotel. Bus stop. Train station. Restaurant. (Late check-in. Rush.
Limited liability.) I'm here at the justice in the eighties conference with
lawyers and judges and other types advocating abbreviating orchestrat-
ing mouthing fucking spilling justice in the bars. Corridors. Bedrooms.
Nothing you'd be interested in. (Luggage received damaged. Torn. Bro-
ken. Scratched. Dented. Lost.) Preparation for the trip to Chestnut
Street. Market Street. Pine Street. Walnut Street. Locust Street. Lom-
bard Street. (Early check-in. Slow and easy liability.) That's why you
missed me at the office. At the office. At the office. It's a deposition. I'm

deposing an entire office of women and other types needing my deposing. Nothing of interest to you. A lot of questions no answers. Long lunches. Laughter. Penises. Flirtings. Touches. Drinks. Cunts and Coke. Jazz and Jacuzzis. *(Morning. Evening. Received. Damaged. Torn. Broken. Dented. Scratched. Lost.)*

> *I shall become a collector of me.*
> ishallbecomeacollectorofme.
> i Shall become a collector of me.
> i shall BECOME a collector of me.
> I shall Become A COLLECTOR of me.
> I SHALL BECOME A COLLECTOR OF ME.
> ISHALLBECOMEACOLLECTOROFME.
> AND PUT MEAT ON MY SOUL.

Part II

I dream of cloisters of marble
when in divine silence,
standing upright, heroes repose:
and at night, in the light of the soul,
I speak to them, in the nighttime!

JOSÉ MARTÍ

Catch the Fire

(Sometimes I Wonder:

    What to say to you now
    in the soft afternoon air as you
    hold us all in a single death?)

I say—

    Where is your fire?

I say—

    Where is your fire?

    You got to find it and pass it on
    You got to find it and pass it on
    from you to me from me to her from her
    to him from the son to the father from the
    brother to the sister from the daughter to
    the mother from the mother to the child.
    Where is your fire? I say where is your fire?
    Can't you smell it coming out of our past?
    The fire of living . . . . . . Not dying
    The fire of loving . . . . . . Not killing
    The fire of Blackness . . . Not gangster shadows.

    Where is our beautiful fire that gave light
    to the world?
    The fire of pyramids;
    The fire that burned through the holes of
    slaveships and made us breathe;
    The fire that made guts into chitterlings;
    The fire that took rhythms and made jazz;

The fire of sit-ins and marches that made
us jump boundaries and barriers;
The fire that took street talk and sounds
and made righteous imhotep raps.
Where is your fire, the torch of life
full of Nzingha and Nat Turner and Garvey
and Du Bois and Fannie Lou Hamer and Martin
and Malcolm and Mandela.

Sister / Sistah. Brother / Brotha. Come / Come.

CATCH YOUR FIRE . . . . DON'T KILL
   HOLD YOUR FIRE . . . . DON'T KILL
   LEARN YOUR FIRE. . . . . DON'T KILL
   BE THE FIRE . . . . DON'T KILL

Catch the fire and burn with eyes
that see our souls:
              WALKING.
              SINGING.
              BUILDING.
              LAUGHING.
              LEARNING.
              LOVING.
              TEACHING.
              BEING.
Hey. Brother / Brotha. Sister / Sistah.
Here is my hand.
Catch the fire . . . and live.
              live.
              livelivelivelive.
              livelivelivelive.
              live.
              live.

A Love Song for Spelman

For Dr. Johnnetta B. Cole and Dr. Camille Cosby

1.

What is a love song for Spelman?
Is it a pulse finding us each day at prayer?
If I am to take one voice which shall it be?
A voice stained like iron, dressed for feminine dreams?
What is a love voice for Spelman?
A song walking in tongues, rising and falling like butterflies?

2.

We begin.
With two women seeing the voice of God in the eyes of Black women.

We begin with newenglandschoolmarms
sisters of silver
creators of light.
Stoking the Southern fires with spit from their White skins.
We begin.

We begin.
With big lips
and dark skins
and woolly hair.
Itinerant eyes in expatriate hearts.
We begin.

We begin.
With a love for freedom
and a thirst for learning.
Tongues heavy with new words
from these our new world lepers.
We begin.

3.

In the long dark basement of shuttered sweat
we sat on benches harder than blue stone.
Some thought us an absurd gathering.
Eleven women of all ages
abundant with mornings.
Hands moving like wings toward knowledge
we came to the basement betrothed to dreams.
And we came to life again.

We came from being not human beings
but hands and feet opening and shutting
in institutionalized work.
We came being not women but trophies
and unremembered bodies hearing our voices in the
delirium of children.

And you told us, O Lord,
that we had to believe that you loved us.
And even though our bodies became stone
we loved you.

4.

We gathered up our skirts, our chins of lard,
from the dark basement to the barracks;
from two teachers to forty-two;
from eleven people to seven hundred;
from one classroom to a campus;
and our breaths agitated rooms and countryside,
became pure and sane and solid and we changed colors
like the seasons and
our hearts burned with fire and
not even the rust of Southern boundaries could stop us.

5.

Like ordained priests: ancient
walking in precise memory.
Like ordained warriors: majestic
Amazon women planting our songs
among the stars and on the waters.
Our songs from farms and cotton fields, from sugar
plantations and slums.
Our songs from urban and suburban roads.
Our songs from Alabama to Georgia, Brazil, and Harlem,
Washington, D.C., and the Congo.
Miracle songs.
Our songs clotting our blood when we bled.
Our songs sweet like eucalyptus against the silence.
Our songs freezing and burning, moving out of corners.
Remaking the air.

6.

Today.
We begin.
A second century of beginnings.
Daughters of great-granddaughters.
Daughters with eyes deeper than flesh.
We begin.
For we are always at the starting point.

We begin
today
with this woman, Johnnetta Cole. A Southern Black
woman.

And we hear her beginning voice
telling us that the dead are never dead.
Their breaths quiver in our shaking hips.
Their voices echo the dew laughing in trees.

We begin
with this woman.
Naming the world as she moves,
"Building for a hundred years hence, not only for today,"
leaving no piece of earth unbaptized.
And we children of all races, daughters from Mozambique
and Soweto, Florida and Mississippi, Cuba and Nicaragua,
outlive our mothers.
And hold our ancestral blood in our hands.

We begin
at this commencement
hearing our foremothers' voices calling to us.
"Listen, Sister Johnnetta. Sister Camille. Spelman sisters.
Listen: They made me give her up. My last child.
He came and took her and i screamed,
called out to Shango and Damballah and Olukun and Jesus
and Massa to jest let me hold on to her a whilst longer.
Just a few mo days til her eyes got usta seein
without me. But they took her anyways. They took her
whilst i wuz praying on my knees, and i walks slowly now,
my feet rooted to this earth, my footsteps echoin her
brown laughter . . ."

We begin today with these women. Camille Cosby and
Johnnetta B. Cole and all these past and present
Spelman women.
Smelling the evening from under the Sun.

We begin as they twist and turn,
as they call out to our Sister Aunties, Sister Mammies,
Sister Mamas, and tell them that their daughters and
sons dance in our veins. They have heard their
daughters' laughter in the wind.

These two women. These Spelman women. Shaping their
passion, involving themselves in work that brings life
to the middle of our stomachs — call out to our
ancestors to us and our children yet to be born.

*Ebe yiye.** *Ebe yiye. Ebe yiye.* For we have the tools now. We have
   the skills and the power. We have the love of self and of our
   people to make it better.
Ebe yiye. Ebe yiye. For you Mama dear. For you Mama Sukey
   moving in and out of plantation doors. For you Mammy
   Teena toiling in the noonday sun. For you young Mama
   strutting you big legs down 125th Street in Harlem. For you
   Lil Bits. Throat cut in a Chicago alley, for a fix.
Ebe yiye because of our love. Our unity, our strength. Our will.
   These two sister women. These Spelman sister women.
   Promise you it'll get better for you and me.
Ebe yiye. Ebe yiye. Ebe yiye. Ebeeee yiyeeee.

We begin.

_____

Ebe yiye: It'll get better.

Poem

What I have seen in the twentieth century is the release of Nelson Mandela from 27 years of imprisonment, fist raised in victory, South African spirit still soaring high;

What I have seen in the twentieth century is Malcolm, hurricane man, shaking us free of our wounds, moving us into the fire that cleanses;

What I have seen in the twentieth century is Fannie Lou Hamer, bathing her flesh in freedom, arresting the old South with her vision for a new South;

What I have seen in the twentieth century is Martin, a nonviolent man silenced by violence, sequestering our eyes on mountaintops;

What I have seen in the twentieth century is the wilderness of African-American women, years trembling like butterflies, traversing the limits of pavements and pain, praising our hands in kitchens and corporations in schools and factories in courtrooms and bedrooms, probing for the peace and beauty and power that are ours;

And today. Walking toward the twenty-first century, with our yesterdays feasting on its past, I move as an African woman, disposed to dreams and truth, disposed to cutting through stone while shaping our laughter like rubies.

Today. My simple passion is to write our names in history and walk in the light that is woman.

Part III

Negritude is what one race

brings to the common rendezvous

where all will strive for the

new world of the poet's vision.

C. L. R. JAMES

Love Song No. 3

1.

i'm crazy bout that chile but she gotta go.
she don't pay me no mind no mo. guess her
mama was right to put her out cuz she
couldn't do nothin wid her. but she been
mine so long. she been my heart so long.
now she breakin it wid her bad habits.
always runnin like a machine out of control;
always lookin like some wild woman trying
to get some place she ain't never been to.
always threatenin me wid her looks.
wid them eyes that don't blink no mo.

i'm crazy bout her though, but she got to go.
her legs walkin with death every day and
one day she gon cross them right in front of
me and one of us will fall.
here she cum openin the do. comin in wid
him. searchin the room with them eyes that
usta smile rivers, searchin for sumthin to
pick up sumthin to put her 18 years into.
how can i keep welcomin her into my house? how
can i put her out the way her mama did
when she 16 years old and fast as lightnin?
she still got baby fat on her cheeks.
still got that smile that'll charm the drawers
off ya. hee hee hee.

2.

it's gittin cold in here. that's a cold
wind she walkin with. that granbaby of mine.
rummagin the house wid her eyes.
rummagin me wid her look.

where you been to girl? been waitin for you
to come home. huh. how you be walter?
you looking better today girl. marlene
baby we need to talk. we need to sit
down and talk bout what you doin
wid yo life. i ain't gon be here forever. but
this money i give you every day.
this money you usin to eat up your bones every day.
this money you need mo of each day is
killin you baby. let me help you outa
this business you done got yo self into.
let me take you to the place miz jefferson
took her son to. you too young and pretty
and smart to just spend yo days walkin
in and out of doors.
yes. i has yo money. yes. i be here when
you come back. but. but. but. alright. Here's
10 dollars. from now on out jest 10 dollars
outa yo mama's insurance money.
that all you need to waste each day on
that stuff. jest 10 dollars. no. i'm not
foolin girl. jest 10 dollars.

3.

what i remember bout her wuz
she was so fat. such a fat baby.
wid smiles. creases. all over her body.

259

her mama had to work weekends
so she stayed wid me and i sang
and played the radio for her and
the smiles multiplied on her body.
jest one big smile she wuz.
harlem ain't no place to raise a
child though, the streets promise so
much but they full of detours fo
young girls wid smiles on they
bodies. i usta sit on the stoop and
watch her jump doubledutch. her
feet bouncin in and out of that
rope like a ballerinas. i could see
two of her inside that rope she
went so fast. multiplyin herself
on these harlem streets outloud. hee hee hee.
she usta run so fast i couldn't get
these old legs of mine to keep up wid her.
i called out: marlene baby. you jest
remember to stop at the corner. you jest
remember to stop fo you git hit by one
of them cars. you jest remember to stop.

4.
Stop it now girl. i ain't studyin you.
stop shovin me. stop it now. you ain't
gittin no mo money. jest the ten dollars.
you got to have sumthin for when you
older. this insurance money your mama
left is you security. yo future.
stop it now girl fo you hurt yoself
help me up offa this floor and put
down that hammer girl. ahahahah.

ahahahahahah. don't hit me no mo marlene.
i got to stand up, move
towards her try to touch her wid these
hands that worked in every house in Bklyn
and Longisland to give her them pretty
dresses she usta wear. heeheehee.
i got to try to turn toward her babyfat.
stop it. marlene. AHAHAHAH.
holy jesus. jesus it hurts. holy jesus.
she see me cryin now she gon stop.
she gon remember when i picked her up from her tricycle
and her head wuz bleedin and i run
her to harlem hospital movin like a madwoman
she gon remember how i held
her tears in my dress.
she gon remember how her arms reached out
to me when the doctor gave her them stitches.
i jest gon reach up to her arm with that hammer.
give me you arms again baby. it's you granmama.
AHAHAHAHAHAHAHAHAHAHAHAH
ohmyjesuswhyhasyouforsakenus?
huh? nobodygonrememberherwhenimgone.
theyonlygonseeherwhitebonesstretchedout
againsttheskynobodygonrememberher
younglegsrunningdownlenoxavenuelessenido
marlenebabygivemeyoarms . . . ahahah.
nobody gon remember me . . .

Introduction of Toni Morrison, and Others, on the Occasion of the Publication of Her Book *Race-ing Justice, En-gendering Power: Essays on Anita Hill, Clarence Thomas, and the Construction of Social Reality*

Of course it ain't strange that you're here in my
bedroom to accept my nomination of you as Supreme
Court Justice. Barb and I both know how important
bedrooms and beds and bathrooms are to you people . . .
Yes indeedy-by-golly-by-gee. . . . What you say Barb?
From the outhouse to the White House;

Of course it ain't strange to this journalist that
you will not be on the golf course when you ascend
to that throne of justice. You (and every other Black man)
know the ball's too small;

Of course it ain't strange for the *New York Times*
to delight in your accomplishment of weight lifting.
We all know that Black men's bodies are important
to them, to women, other men, Phil Donahue, academics,
voyeurs, scientists, journalists, oprahwinfrey, undertakers,
prisons, long winding trees;

Of course it ain't strange for this Senator to love your
laugh, to regard it as "second on my list of the most
fundamental points about Clarence Thomas." Yes indeedy-
by-golly-by-gee. . . . Your smile. Your grin. Your loud
laugh. That comes from deep inside and shakes the body
into an American shuffle stirs the soul and I rest
under this proud tradition of your people;

However, it is strange that this dark vindictive-
looking woman could come charging into these hearings
with her accusations—allegations—of
sexual harassment, sexual misdoings,
sexual intimidation. She is evidently put
up to this by those "special interests" people
or she must be crazy or jealous or deranged or
a scorned lover or jealous or a lesbian or insane
or disturbed or a hater of lighter-complexioned women
or jealous. I mean she wasn't raped or nothing
so what's her problem? Where did this college—law
school—educated witch, this ball busting traitor to the
race, this dumb Black female screwing it up
for all Black males trying to succeed, get on with
this sexual harassment stuff? Where she come
from anyway? Who's her mama?

And it is not strange that Mr. Thomas
was not disqualified immediately at the first
charges leveled against him. I mean, we mean,
what does she mean by sexual harassment, what
does that have to do with work and advancement and
compliance with the rules? After all, doesn't
she know she's Black and female and unmarried
and in need of a job protection advancement verification?
I. We. The men. The country. The world. Have never
heard of a sexually harassed Black woman I don't
care how smart she thinks she is; I mean she's
only a Black woman. Anyone know who's her mama?

Finally it is not strange that we are here with these
"exquisite wordsmiths" who have forged a place for us to
begin to understand the madness of this western psyche,

the madness of men bonding in public against all women.
These writers. These men and women have come to dissect.
Delineate. Decry with brilliance the homicidal nature
of a country that continues to pit Black men and women
in arenas of combat so the executioners can cream
in private with their own pornographic fantasies of how
long and black and how sweetly black it smells.

It is not strange that we have men and women
of conscience here tonite who in defending and
defining Black culture defend the country. The world.
Humanity as well.

So we welcome these wordsmiths. Sister Toni
Morrison. My sister. Sisters Paula Giddings, Nell
Painter, Gayle Pemberton, Kimberlé Crenshaw,
Patricia Williams, Claudia Brodsky Lacour, and
Wahneema Lubiano. And brother Leon
Higginbotham, Jr. My brother. Brothers Cornel
West and Andrew Ross.

And you. My sisters and brothers. This audience
of men/women/students who are here to hear.
Listen.
Listen.
Listen.

Poem for July 4, 1994

For President Václav Havel

1.

It is essential that Summer be grafted to
bones marrow earth clouds blood the
eyes of our ancestors.
It is essential to smell the beginning
words where Washington, Madison, Hamilton,
Adams, Jefferson assembled amid cries of:

> "The people lack information"
> "We grow more and more skeptical"
> "This Constitution is a triple-headed monster"
> "Blacks are property"

It is essential to remember how cold the sun
how warm the snow snapping
around the ragged feet of soldiers and slaves.
It is essential to string the sky
with the saliva of Slavs and
Germans and Anglos and French
and Italians and Scandinavians,
and Spaniards and Mexicans and Poles
and Africans and Native Americans.
It is essential that we always repeat:
> we the people,
> we the people,
> we the people.

2.

"Let us go into the fields" one
brother told the other brother. And

the sound of exact death
raising tombs across the centuries.
Across the oceans. Across the land.

3.
It is essential that we finally understand:
this is the time for the creative
human being
the human being who decides
to walk upright in a human
fashion in order to save this
earth from extinction.

This is the time for the creative
Man. Woman. Who must decide
that She. He. Can live in peace.
Racial and sexual justice on
this earth.

This is the time for you and me.
African American. Whites. Latinos.
Gays. Asians. Jews. Native
Americans. Lesbians. Muslims.
All of us must finally bury
the elitism of race superiority
the elitism of sexual superiority
the elitism of economic superiority
the elitism of religious superiority.

So we welcome you on the celebration
of 218 years Philadelphia. America.

So we salute you and say:
Come, come, come, move out into this world
nourish your lives with a
spirituality that allows us to respect
each other's birth.
come, come, come, nourish the world where
every 3 days 120,000 children die
of starvation or the effects of starvation;
come, come, come, nourish the world
where we will no longer hear the
screams and cries of women, girls,
and children in Bosnia, El Salvador,
Rwanda . . . AhAhAhAh AHAHAHHHHH

Ma-ma. Dada. Mamacita. Baba.
Mama. Papa. Momma. Poppi.
The soldiers are marching in the streets
near the hospital but the nurses say
we are safe and the soldiers are
laughing marching firing calling
out to us i don't want to die i
am only 9 yrs old, i am only 10 yrs old
i am only 11 yrs old and i cannot
get out of the bed because they have cut
off one of my legs and i hear the soldiers
coming toward our rooms and i hear
the screams and the children are
running out of the room i can't get out
of the bed i don't want to die. Don't
let me die Rwanda. America. United
Nations. Don't let me die . . . .

And if we nourish ourselves, our communities
our countries and say

> no more hiroshima
> no more auschwitz
> no more wounded knee
> no more middle passage
> no more slavery
> no more Bosnia
> no more Rwanda

No more intoxicating ideas of
racial superiority
as we walk toward abundance
we will never forget

> the earth
> the sea
> the children
> the people

For *we the people* will always be arriving
a ceremony of thunder
waking up the earth
opening our eyes to human
monuments.
    And it'll get better
    it'll get better
if *we the people* work, organize, resist,
come together for peace, racial, social
and sexual justice
    it'll get better
    it'll get better.

This Is Not a Small Voice

This is not a small voice
you hear   this is a large
voice coming out of these cities.
This is the voice of LaTanya.
Kadesha. Shaniqua. This
is the voice of Antoine.
Darryl. Shaquille.
Running over waters
navigating the hallways
of our schools spilling out
on the corners of our cities and
no epitaphs spill out of their river mouths.

This is not a small love
you hear   this is a large
love, a passion for kissing learning
on its face.
This is a love that crowns the feet with hands
that nourishes, conceives, feels the water sails
mends the children,
folds them inside our history where they
toast more than the flesh
where they suck the bones of the alphabet
and spit out closed vowels.
This is a love colored with iron and lace.
This is a love initialed Black Genius.

This is not a small voice
you hear.

Part IV

I have come to tell you you are beautiful.

I believe you are beautiful,

But that is not the issue.

The issue is they want you dead.

NICOLÁS GUILLÉN

Poem for Some Women

huh?
  i'm all right
  i say i'm
  all right
what you lookin at?
  i say i'm all right
  doing ok
  i'm i'm i'm still
  writin producin on the radio
  who i fooling
  i'm a little ill now
  just got a little jones
      jones jones jones
      habit habit habit

  took my 7 yr old to
  the crack house with me
  on Thursday
  beautiful girl.
  prettiest little girl
  her momma done ever seen
  took her so she understand
  why i'm late sometimes with
  her breakfast dinner bedtime
  meetings bedtime love.
  Wanted her to know how
  hard it is for me you
  know a single woman
  out here on her own you know
  and so i took her to the

crack house where this
man. This dog this
former friend of mine lived
wdn't give me no crack
no action. Even when
i opened my thighs to give him some
him again for the umpteenth
time he sd no all
the while looking at
my baby my pretty
little baby. And he
said i want her. i need
a virgin. Your pussy's
too loose you had
so much traffic up
yo pussy you could
park a truck up there
and still have room
for something else.
And he laughed this long laugh.
And i looked at him and the
stuff he wuz holding in his
hand and you know i cdn't
remember my baby's
name he held the stuff out
to me and i cdn't remember
her birthdate i cdn't remember
my daughter's face. And
i cried as i walked out that door.
    What's her name, puddintang
    ask me again and i'll tell
    you the same thing
cdn't even hear her

screaming my name as he
tore into her pretty little
panties
    "prettiest little girl
    you ever done seen
    prettiest little mama's
    baby you done ever seen."

Bought my baby this pretty
little leather jacket off the street
when i went to pick her up Sunday
7 days later i walked right
up to the house opened the
door and saw her sitting
on the floor she sd Momma
where you been? Momma i
called for you all week
Momma Momma Momma they
hurt me something bad i
want to go home. Momma.

    Momma's little baby
    loves shortening shortening
    Momma's little baby
    loves shortening bread
    put on the jacket
    put on the jacket
    Momma's little baby
    loves shortening bread

When we got home she
wdn't talk to me. She just
sat and stared. Wdn't watch

the t.v. when i turned it on.
When we got home she just
stared at me with her eyes
dog like. Just sat and
looked at me with her eyes til
i had to get outa there
you know.

My baby ran away
from home last week my sweet
little shortening bread ran
away from home last nite and
i dreamed she was dead
i dreamed she was
surrounded by panthers who
tossed her back and forth nibbling
and biting and tearing her up. My little
shortening bread ran away last week
peekaboo i see you and
you and you and you
and you.

haiku 1

i have died and dreamed
myself back to your arms where
what i died for sleeps.

blues haiku 1

all this talk bout love
girl, where you been all your life?
ain't no man can love.

tanka

i have taken five
baths ten showers six shampoos
and still i smell her
scent oozing from the quiet
peeling of our lives.

haiku 2

everywhere i turn
your smile, every room i en/
ter into your smell.

haiku 4

your breath in exile
from me waiting to escape
my persistent air.

haiku 6

if i had known then
what i know now, i would have
picked my own cotton.

sonku

have mercy on the
woman who can't hold
her breath cuz the man's
gon take her for a
long ride to the deep.

South African tanka

the necklace i bring
you is a different one my
love it burns our
history in your flesh it
smells behind the ear of God.

haiku 8

i am hunched down in
veins of fur thick arrows plump
with my depression.

blues haiku 2

ain't no curves in his
talk girl can't trust a man with
no curves on his tongue.

haiku 9

the sprawling sound
of my death sails on the wind
a white butterfly.

from Does Your House Have Lions?

sister's voice

this was a migration unlike
the 1900s of black men and women
coming north for jobs. freedom. life.
this was a migration to begin
to bend a father's heart again
to birth seduction from the past
to repay desertion at last.

imagine him short and black
thin mustache draping thin lips
imagine him country and exact
thin body, underfed hips
watching at this corral of battleships
and bastards. watching for forget
and remember. dancing his pirouette.

and he came my brother at seventeen
recruited by birthright and smell
grabbing the city by the root with clean
metallic teeth. commandant and infidel
pirating his family in their cell
and we waited for the anger to retreat
and we watched him embrace the city and the street.

first he auctioned off his legs. eyes.
heart. in rooms of specific pain.
he specialized in generalize
learned newyorkese and all profane.
enslaved his body to cocaine
denied his father's signature
damned his sister's overture.

and a new geography greeted him.
the atlantic drifted from offshore
to lick his wounds to give him slim
transfusion as he turned changed wore
a new waistcoat of solicitor
antidote to his southern skin
ammunition for a young paladin.

and the bars. the glitter. the light
discharging pain from his bygone anguish
of young black boy scared of the night.
sequestered on this new bank, he surveyed the fish
sweet cargoes crowded with scales feverish
with quick sales full sails of flesh
searing the coastline of his acquiesce.

and the days rummaging his eyes
and the nights flickering through a slit
of narrow bars. hips. thighs.
and his thoughts labeling him misfit
as he prowled, pranced in the starlit
city, coloring his days and nights
with gluttony and praise and unreconciled rites.

brother's voice

father. i despise you for abandoning me
to aunts and mothers and ministers of tissue
tongues, nibbling at my boyish knee.
father. forgive me for i know not what they do
moving me backwards through seams of bamboo
masks, staring eyes campaigning for
my attention. come O lords; my extended metaphor.

sister. i am not your true brother
one half of me resides in my mother's breast
in her eyes where tears exceed their worth.
the other half walks on tiptoe to divest
his tongue of me, this father always a guest
never a permanent resident of my veins
always a traveler to other terrains.

mother. i love you. you are my living saint
walking inside my skull you multiply out loud
in dainty dreams seraphim smiles without a tint
of mystery. you move among us with dark
gait intrepid steps that disavowed
retirement from an elaborate sex
while you prepared each morning's text.

the sermon for each day was my father
husband who left you shipwrecked with child
the movie of the week was my father
staring out from philco screens while your wild
dreams of nouveau lady genuflecting in single file
in a southern city of mouths on mascaraed thighs
twentieth century of elasticized lies.

what does a liver know of peace
or spleen. kidneys. ribs. be still my soul.
how does a city broker its disease
within the confines of a borough, where control
limps tepid—like carrying a parasol
of hurts, hurting, hurted, hurtful croons
stranded in measured arenas without pulpits or spittoons.

came the summer of nineteen sixty
harlem luxuriating in Malcolm's voice
became Big Red beautiful became a city
of magnificent Black Birds steel eyes moist
as he insinuated his words of sweet choice
while politicians complained about this racist
this alchemist. this strategist. this purist.

came the rallies sponsored by new york core
came Malcolm with speeches spilling exact and compact
became a traveling man who revived the poor
who answered with slow echoes became cataract
and fiesta became future and flashback
filling the selves with an old outrage
piercing the cold corners with a new carriage.

then i began an awakening a flowering outside
the living dead became a wanderer of air
barking at the stars became a bride
bridegroom of change timeless black with hair
moist with kinks and morning dare
then i began to think me alive with form and history
then i made my former life an accessory.

how to erect respect in a country of men
where dollars pump their veins?
how to return from exile from swollen
tongues crisscrossing my frail domain?
how to learn to love me amid all the pain?
how to look into his eyes and be reborn
without blood and phlegm and thorn?

from

Like the Singing
Coming off the Drums

Dancing

i dreamt i was tangoing with
you, you held me so close
we were like the singing coming off the drums.
you made me squeeze muscles
lean back on the sound
of corpuscles sliding in blood.
i heard my thighs singing.

Haiku

you ask me to run
naked in the streets with you
i am holding your pulse.

Song

i cannot stay home
on this sweet morning
i must run singing   laughing
through the streets of Philadelphia.
i don't need food or sleep or drink
on this wild scented day
i am bathing in the waves of your breath.

Tanka

i don't know the rules
anymore i don't know if
you say this or not.
i wake up in the nite
tasting you on my breath.

Haiku

i come from the same
place i am going to my
body speaks in tongues.

Haiku

i have caught fire from
your mouth now you want me to
swallow the ocean.

Haiku

for you

love between us is
speech and breath. loving you is
a long river running.

Haiku

i turn westward in
shadows hoping my river
will cross yours in passing.

Sonku

i collect
wings what are
you bird or
animal?
something that
lights on trees
breasts pawnshops
i have seen
another
path to this
rendezvous.

Sonku

1.
i who have
never moved
from where i
was born could
tell you names
dates posit
memory
when you kid
napped my blood
i retired
into my sex.

2.
and i thought
mountains were
men but these
Makonde
Mountains breasts
whispering
spiraling
sound these two
men mountains
long with curves
caress   dance
in a suite
of heavy thighs
sweet mountains
smelling me.

Blues Haiku

you too slippery
for me. can't hold you long or
hard. not enough nites.

Haiku

come windless invader
i am a carnival of
stars a poem of blood.

Haiku

i am moving in
air amazon woman bare
foot thunderbound bells.

Haiku

on passing Toni Cade Bambara's house

how are we here one
day gone the next how do we
run fall down to death?

Blues Haiku

what i need is traveling
minds talktouch kisses spittouch
you swimming upstream.

Haiku

old man standing long
carrying your shanghai years
like an old rickshaw.

Haiku

it is i who have
awakened in nakedness
o cold the morning cock.

Tanka

this man has sucked too
many nipples been inside
too many holes grid
locked too many skins to
navigate a blackwomansail.

Haiku

i am watersnake
crossing your long body
hear me turn in blood.

Haiku

i am the ugly
duckling the second daughter
eyes shaking like leaves.

Haiku

have you ever crossed
the ocean alone seen the
morning cough yellow?

Haiku

mixed with day and sun
i crouched in the earth carry
you like a dark river.

Blues

for Deb

even though you came in december be my january man,
i say, even though you came in december be my january man,
but you know i'll take you any month i can.

woke up this morning, waiting for you to call
say, i woke up this morning waiting for you to call
started shaking in my bed, thought i was taking another fall.

fortune teller, fortune teller, what you forecast for me today,
fortune teller, fortune teller, what you forecast for me today,
cuz i ain't got no time to be messing with yo yesterday.

even though you came in december be my january man,
i say, even though you came in december be my january man,
but you know i'll take you any month i can
but you know i'll take you any month i can.

Haiku

how fast is the wind
sailing? how fast did i go
to become slow?

Blues Haiku

let me be yo wil
derness let me be yo wind
blowing you all day.

Blues Haiku

am i yo philly
outpost? man when you sail in
to my house, you docked.

Haiku

my womb is a dance
of leaves sweating swift winds
i laugh with guitars.

Haiku

for Joanne

sweet woman dancing
your morning sails i see
your riverbound legs.

Poem

1.

i am dreaming
i have spread my dreams out like wings.
i have selected today a dream
about flying and i take off
sailing on your blue smile.
for today it is enough.

2.

all this year
i have heard
my pores
opening.

3.

i have told
you my name
so there is
tomorrow.

4.

see me through
your own eyes
i am here.

5.

let us be one with
the earth expelling anger
spirit unbroken.

6.
we are
only
passing
through let
us touch.

7.
come again inside
me let us take another
turn at loving.

8.
i hear your smell
running across my threshold.
shall i hold your breath?

Sonku

for Nneka and Quincy

love comes with
bone and sea
eyes and rivers
hand of man
tongue of
woman love
trembles at
the edge of
my fingers.

Haiku

c'mon man hold me
touch me before time love me
from behind your eyes.

Tanka

c'mon man ride me
beyond smiles teeth corpuscles
come into my bloodstream
abandon yourself to smell let
us be a call to prayer.

Sonku

i feel your
mouth on my
thighs immac
ulate tongue.

Sonku

i hear the
sound of love
you unstring
like purple beads
over my breasts

Haiku

i am who i am.
nothing hidden just black silk
above two knees.

Haiku

question from a young sister

1.

what's wrong with being
freaky on stage you a stone
freak in yo own skin.

2.

at least we up front
about this freakdom. at least
we let it all hang out.

Poem

Good morning, sex. How do you do?
Tell me how life's been treating you.
You say what? Sex is and sex ain't
sex wuz and sex wuzn't
sex should be and sex has been
on Times Square billboards
on television, in the movies,
in the lyrics dripping off pouting lips.
You say sex is in the drinks we drink
the laughs we laugh
the walk we walk
the smells we smell as we open
our eyes and legs and let the funk spread.
You say sex is dark basements
lights turned out, bodies turned on.
Sex is a breakfast table full of
leftover wine and smiles.
Sex is kinky & clean shaven
sex is straight & gay
sex is do it anyway.
Comes in twos and threes.
Comes on time. Late.
Sex is love. Unlove.
Comes with danger & beauty
Comes in clean and shadowy places.
Sex is life. Death. A gig.
Sometimes you need it in the
Morning. Afternoon. Evening.
Sometimes it satisfies; sometimes it don't

sometimes you feel it in yo' armpits
sometimes you feel it in the mind,
but ah, *ahhh*, when it comes
this sex, when it appears
buck naked or clothed,
when it comes Thelonious Monk–like jazzy,
when it comes hip hopping like the nite
ain't like no other nite; ya
know what time it is, what day
it is, what month it is, what year
it is. When it comes RIGHT, you
understand that sex is & sometimes it ain't
But when it is. . . .

Blues Haiku

for Joanne and Val

yall talkin all under
my clothes bout my love bizness
friends be doin that.

Blues Haiku

i wuz in Kansas
dorothy and toto wuzn't
a jacuzzi. sky. you.

Haiku

i am looking for
you to banish all sermons
a fine hail of touch.

Haiku

these waves boisterous like
Che's mountains smell of mania
howling in my veins.

Haiku

for Louis Massiah

your leonine eyes
squatting in Du Boisian blood.
violets and steel.

Sonku

what is love
you asked
i took you
inside be
hind my eyes
and saw me.

Blues Haiku

my face is a scarred
reminder of your easy
comings and goings.

Haiku

derelict with eyes
i settle in a quiet
carnival of waves.

Haiku

for Queen Mother Moore

they smell like rust
these truants shouting magic
obscure men in heat.

Haiku

a tint on the tongue
an echo in the fingers
i dust off your cough.

Haiku

my teeth can write your
name in hieroglyphics paint
your sound graffiti-like.

Haiku

i have carved your face
on my tongue and i speak you
in my off-key voice.

Sonku

my eyes look
and i don't
see me i
turn around
to find you.

Haiku

i am a small piece
of yellow flesh taking shelter
like a leper.

Haiku

to be lifted in
smoke to be cast in iron
remembering the fire.

Tanka

woman without heat
blankets herself with eyes
avoiding the cock's walk.
a woman in seclusion
dreams of secreting milk.

Haiku

it was nothing big
just no one to put suntan
lotion on my back.

Sonku

what i want
from you can
you give? what
i give to
you do you
want? hey? hey?

Haiku

i hear your breath
in the faraway room
breathing castanets.

Haiku

for Joe Barry

when i imagine
you i recall a river
flowing with eyes.

Haiku

red orange breasts sweet
as chocolate touch my lips
wild bones up for sale

Haiku

and i am flesh burnt
red charcoal black gift wrapped in
philadelphia blood.

Haiku

this poem is for me
who could not speak your death
still i laugh and spin

Short Poem

quite often without
you i am at a loss for
the day.

Haiku 2

my bones migrate in
red noise like pinched wings
they stream white ashes.

Haiku

do you want ashes
where your hands used to be
other faces will come.

Haiku

if i were an old
woman all my veins could hold
my laughter in check.

Haiku

you are rock garden
austere in your loving
in exile from touch.

Tanka

to surround yourself with
arms that will not hold you
to dream yourself home
where the road is dust
and dissolves in purple.

Sonku

to worship
until i
become stone
to love
until i
become bone.

Haiku

my bones hang to
gether like pinched dragonflies
shake loose my skin.

Haiku

for Sophie and Val

in this wet season
of children raining hands
we catch birds in flight.

A Poem for Ella Fitzgerald

when she came on the stage, this Ella
there were rumors of hurricanes and
over the rooftops of concert stages
the moon turned red in the sky,
it was Ella, Ella.

queen Ella had come
and words spilled out
leaving a trail of witnesses smiling
amen—amen—a woman—a woman.

she began
this three agèd woman
nightingales in her throat
and squads of horns came out
to greet her.

streams of violins and pianos
splashed their welcome
and our stained glass silences
our braided spaces
unraveled
opened up
said who's that coming?
who's that knocking at the door?
whose voice lingers on
that stage gone mad with
        perdido. perdido. perdido.
        i lost my heart in toledooooooo.

whose voice is climbing
up this morning chimney
smoking with life
carrying her basket of words
a tisket a tasket
my little yellow
basket—i wrote a
letter to my mom and
on the way i dropped it—
was it red . . . no no no no
was it green . . . no no no no
was it blue . . . no no no no
just a little yellow

voice rescuing razor thin lyrics
from hopscotching dreams.

we first watched her navigating
an apollo stage amid high-stepping
yellow legs
we watched her watching us
shiny and pure woman
sugar and spice woman
her voice a nun's whisper
her voice pouring out
guitar thickened blues,
her voice a faraway horn
questioning the wind,
and she became Ella,
first lady of tongues
Ella cruising our veins
voice walking on water
crossed in prayer,

she became holy
a thousand sermons
concealed in her bones
as she raised them in a
symphonic shudder
carrying our sighs into
her bloodstream.

this voice, chasing the
morning waves,
this Ella-tonian voice soft
like four layers of lace.
> *when i die Ella*
> *tell the whole joint*
> *please, please, don't talk*
> *about me when i'm gone . . .*

i remember waiting one nite
for her appearance
audience impatient at the lateness
of musicians,
i remember it was april
and the flowers ran yellow
the sun downpoured yellow butterflies
and the day was yellow and silent
all of spring held us
in a single drop of blood.

when she appeared on stage
she became Nut arching over us
feet and hands placed on the stage
music flowing from her breasts
she swallowed the sun

sang confessions from the evening stars
made earth divulge her secrets
gave birth to skies in her song
remade the insistent air
and we became anointed found
inside her bop

bop bop dowa

bop bop doowaaa

bop bop dooooowaaaa

Lady. Lady. Lady.
be good. be good
to me.

to you.   to us all
cuz we just some lonesome babes
in the woods
hey lady. sweetellalady
Lady. Lady. Lady. be gooooood
ELLA ELLA ELLALADY

be good

gooooood

gooooooood . . .

Love Poem

for Tupac

1.
we smell the
wounds hear the
red vowels
from your tongue.

the old ones
say we don't
die we are
just passing
through into
another space.

i say they
have tried to
cut out your
heart and eat
it slowly.

we stretch our
ears to hear
your blood young
warrior.

2.
where are your fathers?
i see your mothers gathering
around your wounds folding
your arms shutting your
eyes wrapping you in prayer.

where are the fathers?
zootsuited eyes dancing
their days away.
what have they taught you
about power and peace.

where are the fathers
strutting their furlined
intellect bowing their
faces in the crotch
of academia and corporations
burying their tongues
in lunchtime pink
and black pussies
where are the fathers to teach
beyond stayinschooluse
acondomstrikewhilethe
iron'shotkeephopealive.
where have the fathers buried their voices?

3.
whose gold is carrying you home?
whose wealth is walking you through
this urban terror? whose greed
left you shipwrecked with golden
eyes staring in sudden death?

4.
you were in
a place hot
at the edge
of our minds.
you were in

a new world
a country
pushing with
blk corpses
distinct with
paleness and
it swallowed
you whole.

5.
i will not
burp you up.
i hold you
close to my heart.

For Tupac Amaru Shakur

who goes there? who is this young man born lonely?
who walks there? who goes toward death
whistling through the water
without his chorus? without his posse? without his song?

it is autumn now
in me autumn grieves
in this carved gold of shifting faces
my eyes confess to the fatigue of living.

i ask: does the morning weep for the dead?
i ask: were the bullets conscious atoms entering his chest?
i ask: did you see the light anointing his life?

the day i heard the sound of your death, my brother
i walked outside in the park
we your mothers wanted to see you safely home.
i remembered the poems in your mother's eyes as she
panther-laced warred against the state;
the day you became dust again
we your mothers held up your face green with laughter
and i saw you a child again outside your mother's womb
picking up the harsh handbook of Black life;
the day you passed into our ancestral rivers,
we your mothers listened for your intoxicating voice:
and i heard you sing of tunes bent back in a
cold curse against black
against black (get back)
against black (get back)

we anoint your life
in this absence
we anoint our tongues
with your magic. your genius.
casual warrior of sound
rebelling against humiliation
ayyee—ayyee—ayyee—
i'm going to save these young niggaz
because nobody else want to save them.
nobody ever came to save me. . . .

your life is still warm
on my breath, brother Tupac
Amaru Shakur
and each morning as i
pray for our people
navigating around these
earth pornographers
and each morning when
i see the blue tint of
our Blackness in the
morning dawn
i will call out to you again:

where is that young man born lonely?
and the ancestors' voices will reply:
he is home tattooing his skin with
white butterflies.

and the ancestors will say:
he is traveling with the laughter of trees
his reptilian eyes opening between the blue spaces.

and the ancestors will say:
why do you send all the blessed ones home early?
and the ancestors will say:
you people. Black. lost in the memory of silence.
look up at your children
joined at the spine with death and life.
listen to their genius in a season of dry rain.
listen to them chasing life falling
down getting up in this
house of blue mourning birds.
listen.
& he says: i ain't mad at ya
& we say: so dont cha be mad at yo self
& he says: me against the world
& we say: all of us against the world
& he says: keep yo head up
& we say: yeah family keep yo head up every day
& he says: dear mama, i love you
& we say: dear all the mamas we love you too
& he says: all eyez on me
& we say: kai fi African (come here African)
all eyez on ya from the beginning of time
from the beginning of time
resist.
resist.
resist.
can you say it? resist. resist. resist.
can you say it? resist. resist. resist.
i say. can you do it? resist. resist. resist.
can you rub it into yo sockets? bones?
can you tattoo it on yo body?
so that you see. feel it strengthening you
as you cough blood before the world.

yeah. that's right. write it on your
forehead so you see yourselves as you walk past tomorrow
on your breasts so when
your babies suckle you, when your man woman
taste you they drink the milk of resistance. hee hee hee
take it inside you so when your lover. friend.
companion. enters you they are covered
with the juices, the sweet
cream of resistance. hee hee hee
make everyone who touches this mother lode
a lover of the idea of resistance.
can you say it? RESIST.
can you say it? RESIST.

til it's inside you and you resist
being an electronic nigger hating yo self & me
til you resist lying & gossiping & stealing &
killing each other on every saturday nite corner
til you resist having a baby cuz you want
something to love young sister. love yo self
til you resist being a shonuff stud fuckin
everything in sight, til you resist raping
yo sister, yo wife, somebody's grandmother.
til you resist recolonizing yo mind
mind mind mind mind
resist
resist
resist for Tupac
resist for you & me
reSIST RESIST RESIST
for Brother
Tupac
Amaru
Shakur

from Remembering and Honoring Toni Cade Bambara

how to respond to the genius
of our sister Toni Cade Bambara? How to
give praise to this brilliant. Hard. Sweet
talking Toni. Who knew everything.
Read everything. Saw everything?

I guess if we remember Willie Kgositsile's lines:

if you sing of workers you have praised her
if you sing of brotherhood and sisterhood you
have praised her
if you sing of liberation you have praised her
if you sing of peace you have praised her
you have praised her without knowing
her name
her name is Spear of the Nation . . .

I would also add:

her name is clustered on the hills
for she has sipped at the edge of rivers
her words have the scent of the earth
and the genius of the stars
i have stored in my blood the
memory of your voice Toni linking continents
making us abandon Catholic minds.
You spread yourself rainbowlike
across seas
Your voice greeting foreign trees
Your voice stalking the evening stars.

. . . .

. . . .

What we know today is that this
earth cannot support murderers,
imperialists, rapists, racists, sexists,
homophobes. This earth cannot
support those who would invent
just for the sake of inventing
and become death.

We must all say i have
become life, look at me
i have become life
i move like the dawn with a tint of
blue in my hair
i say, i say
i have become life and
i walk a path that clears
away the debris of
pornographers.
i have become life, light,
life, light, life,
light and i move
with my eyes
My hands holding up life
for the world.
i have become life . . .

For Sister Gwen Brooks

you tell the stars
don't be jealous of her light
you tell the ocean,
you call out to Olukun,
to bring her always to
safe harbor,
for she is a holy one
this woman twirling
her emerald lariat
you tell the night
to move gently
into morning so she's
not startled,
you tell the morning
to ease her into a water
fall of dreams
for she is a holy one
restringing her words
from city to city
so that we live and
breathe and smile and
breathe and love and
breath her . . .
this Gwensister called life.

13

from

Shake Loose My Skin

Morning Song
and Evening Walk

1.
Tonite in need of you
and God
I move imperfect
through this ancient city.

Quiet. No one hears
No one feels the tears
of multitudes.

The silence thickens
I have lost the shore
of your kind seasons
who will hear my voice
nasal against distinguished
actors.

O I am tired
of voices without sound
I will rest on this ground
full of mass hymns.

2.
You have been here since I can remember Martin
from Selma to Montgomery from Watts to Chicago
from Nobel Peace Prize to Memphis, Tennessee.
Unmoved among the angles and corners
of aristocratic confusion.

It was a time to be born
forced forward a time
to wander inside drums
the good times with eyes like stars
and soldiers without medals or weapons
but honor, yes.

And you told us: *the storm is rising against the*
privileged minority of the earth, from which there is no
shelter in isolation or armament
and you told us: the storm will
not abate until a just distribution of the fruits of
the earth enables men (and women) everywhere to live
in dignity and human decency.

3.
All summerlong it has rained
and the water rises in our throats
and all that we sing is rumored
forgotten.
Whom shall we call when this song comes of age?
And they came into the city carrying their fastings
in their eyes and the young 9-year-old Sudanese
boy said, "I want something to eat at nite a
place to sleep."
And they came into the city hands salivating guns,
and the young 9-year-old words snapped red
with vowels:
Mama mama Auntie auntie I dead I dead I deaddddd.

4.

In our city of lost alphabets
where only our eyes strengthen the children
you spoke like Peter like John
you fisherman of tongues
untangling our wings
you inaugurated iron for our masks
exiled no one with your touch
and we felt the thunder in your hands.

We are soldiers in the army
we have to fight, although we have to cry.
We have to hold up the freedom banners
we have to hold it up until we die.

And you said we must keep going and we became
small miracles, pushed the wind down, entered
the slow bloodstream of America
surrounded streets and "reconcentradas," tuned
our legs against Olympic politicians elaborate cadavers
growing fat underneath western hats.
And we scraped the rust from old laws
went floor by floor window by window
and clean faces rose from the dust
became new brides and bridegrooms among change
men and women coming for their inheritance.
And you challenged us to catch up with our
own breaths to breathe in Latinos Asians Native Americans
Whites Blacks Gays Lesbians Muslims and Jews, to gather
up our rainbow-colored skins in peace and racial justice
as we try to answer your long-ago question: Is there
a nonviolent peacemaking army that can shut down
the Pentagon?

And you challenged us to breathe in Bernard Haring's words:
the materialistic growth—mania for
more and more production and more
and more markets for selling unnecessary
and even damaging products is a
sin against the generation to come
what shall we leave to them:
rubbish, atomic weapons numerous
enough to make the earth
uninhabitable, a poisoned
atmosphere, polluted water?

5.
"Love in practice is a harsh and dreadful
thing compared to love in dreams," said a Russian writer.
Now I know at great cost Martin that as we burn
something moves out of the flames
(call it spirit or apparition)
till no fire or body or ash remain
we breathe out and smell the world again
Aye-Aye-Aye Ayo-Ayo-Ayo Ayeee-Ayeee-Ayeee
Amen men men men Awoman woman woman woman
Men men men Woman woman woman
Men men Woman woman
Men Woman
Womanmen.

For Sweet Honey in the Rock

I'm gonna stay on the battlefield
I'm gonna stay on the battlefield
I'm gonna stay on the battlefield til I die.

I'm gonna stay on the battlefield
I'm gonna stay on the battlefield
I'm gonna stay on the battlefield til I die.

i had come into the city carrying life in my eyes
amid rumors of death,
calling out to everyone who would listen
it is time to move us all into another century
time for freedom and racial and sexual justice
time for women and children and men time for hands unbound
i had come into the city wearing peaceful breasts
and the spaces between us smiled
i had come into the city carrying life in my eyes.
i had come into the city carrying life in my eyes.

And they followed us in their cars with their computers
and their tongues crawled with caterpillars
and they bumped us off the road turned over our cars,
and they bombed our buildings killed our babies,
and they shot our doctors maintaining our bodies,
and their courts changed into confessionals
but we kept on organizing we kept on teaching believing
loving doing what was holy moving to a higher ground
even though our hands were full of slaughtered teeth
but we held out our eyes delirious with grace.
but we held out our eyes delirious with grace.

I'm gonna treat everybody right
I'm gonna treat everybody right
I'm gonna treat everybody right til I die.

I'm gonna treat everybody right
I'm gonna treat everybody right
I'm gonna treat everybody right til I die.

come. i say come, you sitting still in domestic bacteria
come. i say come, you standing still in double-breasted mornings
come. i say come, and return to the fight.
this fight for the earth
this fight for our children
this fight for our life
we need your hurricane voices
we need your sacred hands

i say, come, sister, brother to the battlefield
come into the rain forests
come into the hood
come into the barrio
come into the schools
come into the abortion clinics
come into the prisons
come and caress our spines

i say come, wrap your feet around justice
i say come, wrap your tongues around truth
i say come, wrap your hands with deeds and prayer
you brown ones
you yellow ones
you black ones

you gay ones
you white ones
you lesbian ones

Comecomecomecomecome to this battlefield
called life, called life, called life. . . .

I'm gonna stay on the battlefield
I'm gonna stay on the battlefield
I'm gonna stay on the battlefield til I die.

I'm gonna stay on the battlefield
I'm gonna stay on the battlefield
I'm gonna stay on the battlefield til I die.

Aaaayeee Babo (Praise God)

1.

There are women sailing the sky
I walk between them
They who wear silk, muslin and burlap skins touching mine
They who dance between urine and violets
They who are soiled disinherited angels with masculine eyes.

This earth is hard symmetry
This earth of feverish war
This earth inflamed with hate
This patch of tongues corroding the earth's air.
Who will journey to the place we require of humans?
I grow thin on these algebraic equations reduced to a final
   common denominator.

2.

I turn away from funerals from morning lightning
I feast on rain and laughter
What is this sound I hear moving through our bones
I breathe out leaving our scent in the air.

3.

I came to this life with serious hands
I came observing the terrorist eyes moving in and out of
   Southern corners
I wanted to be the color of bells
I wanted to surround trees and spill autumn from my fingers
I came to this life with serious feet—heard other footsteps
   gathering around me
Women whose bodies exploded with flowers.

4.
Life.
Life is
from curled embryo
to greed
to flesh
transistors
webpages obscuring butterflies.

Our life
is a feast of flutes
orbiting chapels
no beggar women here
no treasonous spirit here
just a praise touch
created from our spirit tongues
We bring the noise of mountain language
We bring the noise of Sunday mansions
We enter together paddling a river of risks
in order to reshape This wind, This sea,
This sky, This dungeon of syllables
We have become nightingales singing us out of fear
Splashing the failed places with light.

We are here.
On the green of leaves
On the shifting waves of blues,
Knowing once that our places divided us
Knowing once that our color divided us
Knowing once that our class divided us
Knowing once that our sex divided us
Knowing once that our country divided us
Now we carry the signature of women in our veins
Now we build our reconciliation canes in morning fields

Now the days no longer betray us
and we ascend into wave after wave of our blood milk.
What can we say without blood?

5.

Her Story.
Herstory smiles at us.
Little by little we shall interpret the decorum of peace
Little by little we shall make circles of these triangular stars
We Shall strip-mine the world's eyes of secrets
We shall gather up our voices
Braid them into our flesh like emeralds
Come. Bring us all the women's hands
Let us knead calluses into smiles
Let us gather the mountains in our children's eyes
Distill our unawakened love
Say hello to the mangoes
    the uninformed men
    the nuns
    the prostitutes
    the rainmothers
    the squirrels
    the clouds
    the homeless.
Come. Celebrate our footsteps insatiable as sudden breathing
Love curves the journey of these women sails
Love says Awoman. Awoman to these tongues of thunder

Come celebrate this prayer
I bring to our common ground.
It is enough
to confound the conquistadores
it is enough to shape our lace,
our name.

Make us become healers
Come celebrate the poor
the women
the gays
the lesbians
the men
the children
the black, brown, yellow, white
Sweat peeling with stories

Aaaaayeee babo.
I spit on the ground
I spit language on the dust
I spit memory on the water
I spit hope on this seminary
I spit teeth on the wonder of women, holy volcanic women
Recapturing the memory of our most sacred sounds.

Come
where the drum speaks
come tongued by fire and water and bone
come praise God and
Ogun and Shango and
Olukun and Oya and
Jesus
Come praise our innocence
our decision to be human
reenter the spirit of morning doves
and our God is near
I say our God is near
I say our God is near
Aaaayeee babo Aaaayeee babo Aaaayeee babo
(Praise God).

Fragment 1

alone
deranged by loitering
i hear the bricks pacing my window.
my pores know how to come.
what survives in me
i still suspect.

how still this savior.
white suit in singing hand.
spitting mildew air.
who shapes the shade
is.

i am a reluctant ache
authenticating my bones.
i shall spread out my veins
and beat the dust into noise.

Fragment 2

I am reciting the rain
caught in my scream.
these lips cannot swim
only by breasts wild as
black waves.

I met a collector of rain   once
who went to sleep in my sleeve.
is his alibi still under
my arm?

I keep coughing up butterflies
my entrails trail albino tunes
his voice comes in my hair.
is the flesh tender where the knees weep?

Haiku

man. you write me so
much you bad as the loanhouse
asking fo they money

Towhomitmayconcern

watch out fo the full moon of sonia

shinin down on ya.

git yo/self fattened up man

you gon be doing battle with me

ima gonna stake you out

grind you down

leave greasy spots all over yo/soul

till you bone dry. man.

you gon know you done been touched by me

this time.

ima gonna tattoo me on you fo ever

leave my creases all inside yo creases

i done warned ya boy

watch out

for the full moon of sonia

shinin down on ya.

Song No. 2

(1)

i say. all you young girls waiting to live
i say. all you young girls taking yo pill
i say. all you sisters tired of standing still
i say. all you sisters thinkin you won't, but you will.

don't let them kill you with their stare
don't let them closet you with no air
don't let them feed you sex piecemeal
don't let them offer you any old deal.

i say. step back sisters. we're rising from the dead
i say. step back johnnies. we're dancing on our heads
i say. step back man. no mo hangin by a thread
i say. step back world. can't let it all go unsaid.

(2)

i say. all you young girls molested at ten
i say. all you young girls giving it up again & again
i say. all you sisters hanging out in every den
i say. all you sisters needing your own oxygen.

don't let them trap you with their coke
don't let them treat you like one fat joke
don't let them bleed you till you broke
don't let them blind you in masculine smoke.

i say. step back sisters. we're rising from the dead
i say. step back johnnies. we're dancing on our heads
i say. step back man. no mo hanging by a thread.
i say. step back world. can't let it go unsaid.

An Anthem

for the ANC and Brandywine Peace Community

Our vision is our voice
we cut through the country
where madmen goosestep in tune to Guernica.

we are people made of fire
we walk with ceremonial breaths
we have condemned talking mouths.

we run without legs
we see without eyes
loud laughter breaks over our heads.

give me courage so I can spread
it over my face and mouth.

we are secret rivers
with shaking hips and crests
come awake in our thunder
so that our eyes can see behind trees.

for the world is split wide open
and you hide your hands behind your backs
for the world is broken into little pieces
and you beg with tin cups for life.

are we not more than hunger and music?
are we not more than harlequins and horns?
are we not more than color and drums?
are we not more than anger and dance?

give me courage so I can spread it
over my face and mouth.

we are the shakers
walking from top to bottom in a day
we are like Shango
involving ourselves in acts
that bring life to the middle
of our stomachs

we are coming towards you madmen
shredding your death talk
standing in front with mornings around our waist
we have inherited our prayers from
the rain
our eyes from the children of Soweto.

red rain pours over the land
and our fire mixes with the water.

give me courage so I can spread
it over my face and mouth.

from

Morning Haiku

haikuography

From the moment i found a flowered book high up on a shelf at the 8th Street Bookshop in New York City, a book that *announced* Japanese haiku; from the moment i opened that book, and read the first haiku, i slid down onto the floor and cried and was changed. i had found *me*. It's something to find yourself in a poem—to discover the beauty that i knew resided somewhere in my twenty-one-year-old bloodstream; from the moment i asked the clerk in the bookstore if i was pronouncing this haiku word correctly, i knew that i had discovered me, had found an awakening, an awareness that i was connected not only to nature, but to the nature of myself and others; from the moment i saw the blood veins behind beautiful eyes, the fluids in teeth, and the enamel in tongues, i knew that haiku were no short-term memory, but a long memory.

Patricia Donegan shares the idea of "haiku mind"—"a simple yet profound way of seeing our everyday world and living our lives with the awareness of the moment expressed in haiku—and to therefore hopefully inspire others to live with more clarity, compassion, and peace."

i knew when i heard young poets say in verse and conversation: i'm gonna put you on "pause," i heard their "haiku nature," their haikuography. They were saying, i gotta make you slow down and check out what's happening in your life. In the world.

So this haiku slows us down, makes us stay alive and breathe with that one breath that it takes to recite a haiku.

This haiku, this tough form disguised in beauty and insight, is like the blues, for they both offer no solutions, only a pronouncement, a formal declaration—an acceptance of pain, humor, beauty and non-beauty, death and rebirth, surprise and life. Always life. Both always help us to maintain memory and dignity.

What i found in the 8th Street Bookshop was extraordinary and *ordinary*: Silence. Crystals. Cornbread and greens. Laughter. Brocades. The sea. Beethoven. Coltrane. Spring and winter. Blue rivers. Dreadlocks. Blues. A waterfall. Empty mountains. Bamboo. Bodegas. Ancient generals. Lamps. Fireflies. Sarah Vaughan—her voice exploding in the universe, returning to earth in prayer. Plum blossoms. Silk and steel. *Cante jondo*. Wine. Hills. Flesh. Perfume. A breath inhaled and held. Silence.

And i found that my mouth and the river are one and the same.

i set sail

in tall grass

no air stirs.

10 haiku

for Max Roach

Nothing ends
every blade of grass
remembering your sound

your sounds exploding
in the universe return
to earth in prayer

as you drummed
your hands kept
reaching for God

the morning sky
so lovely imitates
your laughter

you came warrior
clear your music
kissing our spines

feet tapping
singing, impeach
our blood

you came drumming
sweet life on
sails of flesh

your fast beat
riding the air settles
in our bones

your drums
soloing our breaths into
the beat . . . unbeat

your hands
shimmering on the
legs of rain.

dance haiku

Do we dance
death in a fast lane
of salsa

or minuet
death with an aristocrat's
pointed toe

do we ease
into death with
workingclass abandon

or position our
legs in middleclass
laughter

do we swallow
death in a fast gulp
of morning pills

or factor death
into prime years
in our throats?

14 haiku

for Emmett Louis Till

Your limbs buried
in northern muscle carry
their own heartbeat

Mississippi . . .
alert with
conjugated pain

young Chicago
stutterer whistling
more than flesh

your pores
wild stars embracing
southern eyes

footprints blooming
in the night remember
your blood

in this southern
classroom summer settles
into winter

i hear your
pulse swallowing
neglected light

your limbs
fly off the ground
little birds . . .

we taste the
blood ritual of
southern hands

blue midnite
breaths sailing on
smiling tongues

say no words
time is collapsing
in the woods

a mother's eyes
remembering a cradle
pray out loud

walking in Mississippi
i hold the stars
between my teeth

your death
a blues, i could not
drink away.

from **21 haiku**

for Odetta

The sound of
your voice thundering out
of the earth

a drum
beat summoning us
to prayer

behold
the smell of
your breathing

dilated
by politics
you dared to love

your music asked:
has your song a father
or a mother?

on stage
you were a
soldier of hands

accenting
beat after beat
into beauty

your songs journeyed
in a country padlocked
with greed

a country
still playing on
adolescent knees

finally we remember
how you gave life
to memory

remember your eyes
morning stars
perfumed with rain

your mouth
a sweet wind
painted with hieroglyphics

finally to pass
your song into our
ancestral rivers.

4 haiku

for Max Roach

i need to
catch your brain
and steady it

let's impeach
this yellow detour
of your memory

how dare
your sweet hands
forget you!

i kiss the
surprise always in
your eyes.

sister haiku

for Pat

How many
secrets you carried
in your panties

infections
of confections
no retractions

the autumnal
rain announced a
sister's fragrance

your slanted
black eyes smiled
crystals

can two little
girls holding hands walk unnoticed
in a large house?

young man . . . home from war . . .
envies the subtle
pause of young beauty

disguised as
uncle he picked at
your unbroken spine

how to moisten
the silence of an
afternoon molestation?

silk on your
skin no armor for
the amputee

Birmingham
eyes ignoring
the winter's confinement

to be born
to be raped
each journey a sudden wave

his touch wore
you down to a
fugitive eye.

the sound of you
sucking your thumb at nite
blows in my ears

all morning
our mother's voice
beyond the hills.

15 haiku

for Toni Morrison

We know so little
about migrations of souls crossing
oceans. seas of longing;

      we have not always been
      prepared for landings that held
      us suspended above our bones;

      in the beginning
      there wuz we and they and others
      too mournful to be named;

or brought before elders
even held in contempt. they were
so young in their slaughterings;

in the beginning
when memory was sound. there was
bonesmell. bloodtear. whisperscream;

and we arrived
carrying flesh and disguise
expecting nothing;

always searching
for gusts of life
and sermons;

in the absence
of authentic Gods
new memory;

in our escape from plunder
in our nesting on agitated land
new memory;

in our fatigue at living
we saw mountains cracking
skulls, purple stars, colourless nights;

trees praising our innocence
new territories dressing our
limbs in starched bones;

in our traveling to weselves
in the building, in the journeying
to discover our own deaths;

in the beginning
there was a conspiracy of blue eyes
to iron eyes;

new memory falling into death
O will we ever know
what is no more with us;

O will weselves ever
convalesce as we ascend into wave after
wave of bloodmilk?

6 haiku

for Elizabeth Catlett in Cuernavaca

La Señora
making us remember
flesh and wind

O how you
help us catch
each other's breath

a woman's
arms climbing with
colored dreams

Elizabeth
slides into the pool
hands kissing the water

i pick
up your breath and
remember me

your hands
humming hurricanes
of beauty.

2 haiku

for Ras Baraka

Your hands
shout eucalyptus
songs

your poems
the smell of
morning rain.

5 haiku

for Sarah Vaughan

Me in midair
sailing underneath
your lips.

we don't stare
we don't seem to care
are we a pair?

where are the clowns
are they all stampeding
my house?

without your
residential breath
i lose my timing.

Send in the clowns
There is space
above the air.

9 haiku

for Freedom's Sisters

(Kathleen Cleaver)
> quicksilver
> panther woman speaking
> in thunder

(Charlayne Hunter-Gault)
> summer silk woman
> brushing the cobwebs
> off Southern legs

(Shirley Chisholm)
> We saw your
> woman sound   footprinting
> congressional hallways

(Betty Shabazz)
> your quiet face
> arrived at a road
> unafraid of ashes . . .

(Fannie Lou Hamer)
> feet deep
> in cotton you shifted
> the country's eyes

(Barbara Jordan)
> Texas star
> carrying delicate words
> around your waist

(Rosa Parks)
> baptizer of
> morning light walking us away
> from reserved spaces

(Myrlie Evers-Williams)
> you rescued women and men
> from southern subscriptions
> of death

(Dr. Dorothy Irene Height)
> I
> your words
> helped us reconnoiter
> the wonder of women

> II
> woman sequestered
> in the hurricane
> of herstory . . .

5 love haiku

Under
a sexual sky you
coughed swords

your smell
slides under my
fingernails

love
walking backwards
towards assassinations

locust man
eating the grain
of women

your tongue
jelly on my
lips.

6 haiku

for Maya Angelou

You have
taught us how
to pray

your poems
yellow tattoos on the
morning dew

we dance
in the eye
of your pores

in a sudden
pause of breath
secrets unlock

you show us
how to arrange our
worldly selves

your poems
a landscape of
seabirds.

memory haiku

i was born
a three-legged
black child.

carrying an
extra leg for quick
departures.

beneath the sun
i moved in short
Birmingham breaths.

silence of the
house . . . in the kitchen
someone washes the floor.

silence. no words.
just the sound
of earthquakes.

precocious morning
releasing an avalanche
of blood.

in the hospital
mother, you chanted complex
half-moons.

what is it about
childbirth that women
ask for seconds?

how long the nite
to break your body into
a diabetic coma.

how wild the
gust of blood running
down hospital corridors.

do women
make a living singing
death prints?

in my dreams
i rubbed your limbs
until they sparkled.

wherever i am
i patrol
your seasonal death.

i bring you
pine trees and laughter
for your journey.

do you hear me
singing in the mountains
under a constant sky?

i, a passerby
to your death,
cradle your breath.

i, a sleepwalker
to dreams, imagine you a
crane flying south.

every day
i hear your voice
beyond the hills.

haiku poem: 1 year after 9/11

Sweet September morning
how did you change skirts so fast?

What is the population of death
at 8:45 on a Tuesday morning?

How does a country become
an orphan to its own blood?

Will these public deaths
result in private bloodletting?

Amongst the Muslim, the Jew, and the Christian
whom does God love more?

How did you disappear, peace, without
my shawl to accompany you?

What *cante jondo* comes
from a hijacked plane?

Did you hear the galvanized steel
thundering like hunted buffalo?

Glass towers collapsing in prayer
are you a permanent guest of God?

Why do some days wear the
clothing of a beggar?

Where did these pornographic flames
come from, blaspheming sealed births?

Did they search for pieces of life
by fingerprinting the ash?

Death speaking in a loud voice,
are your words only for the deaf?

What is the language for bones
scratching the air?

What is the accent of life
when windows reflect only death?

Hey death! You furious frequent flier,
can you hear us tasting this earth?

Did the currents recognize her sound
as she sailed into the clouds?

Does death fly south
at the end of the day?

Did you see the burnt bones
sleepwalking a city?

Is that Moses. Muhammad. Buddha. Jesus.
gathering up the morning dead?

Why did you catch them, death,
holding their wings out to dry?

How did this man become
a free-falling soliloquy?

Why did September come whistling
through the air in a red coat?

How hard must the wind
blow to open our hearts?

How to reconnoiter our lives
away from epileptic dreams?

How to live—How to live
without contraband blood?

Is this only an eastern wind
registering signatures of ash?

Do the stars genuflect
with pity toward everyone?

Envoi:
For Harriet Tubman

Haiku and Tanka
for Harriet Tubman

1

Picture a woman
riding thunder on
the legs of slavery . . .

2

Picture her kissing
our spines saying *no* to
the eyes of slavery . . .

3

Picture her rotating
the earth into a shape
of lives becoming . . .

4

Picture her leaning
into the eyes of our
birth clouds . . .

5

Picture this woman
saying *no* to the constant
yes of slavery . . .

6

Picture a woman
jumping rivers her
legs inhaling moons . . .

7
Picture her ripe
with seasons of
legs . . . running . . .

8
Picture her tasting
the secret corners
of woods . . .

9
Picture her saying:
You have within you the strength,
the patience, and the passion
to reach for the stars,
to change the world . . .

10
Imagine her words:
Every great dream begins
with a dreamer . . .

11
Imagine her saying:
I freed a thousand slaves,
could have freed
a thousand more if they
only knew they were slaves . . .

12
Imagine her humming:
How many days we got
fore we taste freedom . . .

13
Imagine a woman
asking: *How many workers*
for this freedom quilt . . .

14
Picture her saying:
A live runaway could do
great harm by going back
but a dead runaway
could tell no secrets . . .

15
Picture the daylight
bringing her to woods
full of birth moons . . .

16
Picture John Brown
shaking her hands three times saying:
General Tubman. General Tubman. General Tubman.

17
Picture her words:
There's two things I got a
right to: death or liberty . . .

18
Picture her saying *no*
to a play called *Uncle Tom's Cabin*:
I am the real thing . . .

19
Picture a Black woman:
could not read or write
trailing freedom refrains . . .

20
Picture her face
turning southward walking
down a Southern road . . .

21
Picture this woman
freedom bound . . . tasting a
people's preserved breath . . .

22
Picture this woman
of royalty . . . wearing a crown
of morning air . . .

23
Picture her walking,
running, reviving
a country's breath . . .

24
Picture black voices
leaving behind
lost tongues . . .

25
Picture her
Painting rainbows on
A summerbent people

26
Picture a woman
Walking on freedom legs
A seaspray of life

About the Author

Poet, playwright, educator, and activist **SONIA SANCHEZ** is one of the founders of the Black Arts movement. She is the author of more than a dozen books of poetry, most represented here. *Does Your House Have Lions?* was nominated for both the NAACP Image and the National Book Critics Circle Award; *Homegirls & Handgrenades* won an American Book Award from the Before Columbus Foundation. She is also the author of several acclaimed plays, a collection of prose writing, and books for children.

Among the hundreds of honors she has received are the Robert Creeley Award, the Frost Medal, the Community Service Award from the National Black Caucus of State Legislators, the Lucretia Mott Award, the Outstanding Arts Award from the Pennsylvania Coalition of 100 Black Women, the Peace and Freedom Award from the Women's International League for Peace and Freedom, the Pennsylvania Governor's Award for Excellence in the Humanities, a National Endowment for the Arts Award, and a Pew Fellowship in the Arts. In 2018, she received the Wallace Stevens Award, given annually to recognize outstanding and proven mastery in the art of poetry, and in 2019, the prestigious Anisfield-Wolf Lifetime Achievement award.

Professor Sanchez has lectured at more than five hundred universities and colleges in the United States and has traveled extensively, reading her poetry in many countries around the world. She was the first Presidential Fellow at Temple University, where she began teaching in 1977, and held the Laura Carnell Chair in English there until her retirement in 1999. Born in Birmingham, and having spent years in Harlem, Sonia Sanchez now lives in Philadelphia.